MR SMILEY

Also by Howard Marks

MR NICE

THE HOWARD MARKS BOOK OF DOPE STORIES

SEÑOR NICE

HOWARD MARKS

MR SMILEY
MY LAST PILL AND TESTAMENT

MACMILLAN

First published 2015 by Macmillan
an imprint of Pan Macmillan
20 New Wharf Road, London N1 9RR
Associated companies throughout the world
www.panmacmillan.com

ISBN 978-1-5098-0966-0 HB
ISBN 978-1-5098-0967-7 TPB

Visit **www.panmacmillan.com** to read more about all our books
and to buy them. You will also find features, author interviews and
news of any author events, and you can sign up for e-newsletters
so that you're always first to hear about our new releases.

*The names of some individuals in this book
have been changed.*

'I was looking for something hidden, for someone who didn't want to be found, it was that oldest sort of trouble.'

Falling Angel, William Hjortsberg
(adapted into the film *Angel Heart*)

'We had a dream,
and the gangsters made a killing.'

Tony Wilson,
in conversation with Howard Marks

This book is dedicated to my daughter
Myfanwy Marks

On the last day of 1996, less than two years after I had been released early for good behaviour from a twenty-five-year sentence in United States Penitentiary, Terre Haute, for drug smuggling, I found myself carrying a packet of extremely pure MDMA through an airport. Of course they had a sniffer dog on me as soon as I got to Customs at Palma de Mallorca. The decision as to who to search is usually made in advance on the basis of the passenger list and, as I was travelling from London under my own name, I had expected trouble. I had also watched the chaos that had unfolded that year as the airport was renovated and so, after I was waved through passport control I had snuck into a storage area I knew was accessible to the public. As I was ushered into a cubicle by a two-man search team, the packet of MDMA was in another part of the airport, stuck in beeswax on the inside of a cupboard door.

After they'd searched me and found nothing, somewhat grudgingly they let me go. Some ground staff and cleaners were smoking in the doorways; they glanced at me as I made my way back between the sheds to where the buses were parked, but said nothing. I looked back at the main building, as if that was where I was going, and pulling on some overalls from my bag, doubled back, out of sight of the terminal windows.

The packet was where I had left it, stuck on the inside of the cupboard door, in a building used by the Spanish charter line Aviaco. Putting it in my trouser pocket, I felt the sticky weight of it rubbing against my leg, and now the crowds through the windows in the transit lounge no longer troubled me. The open spaces seemed small and unintimidating. For the first time since leaving prison, I felt whole and in control again.

It was futile to deny my true nature: as a true runner is born to run, and a writer to write, the smuggler's buzz would always be there, deep in my being, like a retrovirus ready to be awoken, and any other life would probably never satisfy, and now it seemed important – though I cannot say exactly why – to mark this apparent moment of revelation in some indelible way and, as I drove out, passing a roadside Madonna, I pulled over.

This was on one of the shortcuts through the outer suburbs of Palma. It was almost night now, and I could barely see her features. Getting out, crouching in the roadside, already feeling a little apprehensive as I did so, I made a solemn oath that I would return to being true to *myself before the year was out; but hardly had I finished than the air around me seemed to be filled with coarse, cackling laughter, and strangely, looking around, I could not see its source, as though it emanated from the image itself. Probably it came from a neighbouring building, or a nearby car, but it felt as if it were directed at me alone.*

In town my daughters, Amber and Francesca, were waiting for me at a bar. The girls seemed as beautiful and assured as ever, no less so than in those first weeks after my return: both had come through my prison-years stronger and more knowing than I could ever have hoped, and sitting there, the weight of the oath hung over me, feeling, by the minute, more like a curse than something I really wanted.

After eighteen months of trying to work out what sort of life, if any, was left for me after seven years in prison, I was returning from a series of events in Britain to publicize my memoir Mr Nice, *and though it seemed in some ways as if my prospects were brightening, I couldn't escape the sense that something important was missing.*

I must have been unusually quiet because the girls kept giving me concerned looks and were trying to break the ice with chat about music, the only topic which always got me talking. In prison, the music on the radio had been country, and in the black-dominated dayroom there had only been hip-hop, but now Francesca was trying to turn me onto trance and acid house. The point she kept returning to was that this music made no sense unless one was on ecstasy when one listened, and it was apparent from the way she talked that she was already familiar with the drug, and she told me that there was a rave – something I'd had no experience of – in the cave at Gal Dent, a forty-minute drive away from Palma, in the mountains near Llucmajor, and that was where we were heading.

As the midnight hour was striking, with a glass of cava in one hand and a joint in the other, I kissed my children and, as is the Spanish custom, spat out a grape pip for each year of my life I had spent behind bars. As the moment came to make resolutions, my mind was still suffused with the Madonna, whose face I had not seen clearly. The words of my oath, and the cackling laughter that had followed, still echoed around my head.

I knew my wish should be to undo the oath I had made. But the moment passed before I had wished, and it was too late. As we reached the mountains, the beauty of the place began to make me forget what had happened; the first hints of dawn-light filling the air; the winter sky seeming to burn with ethereal pinks and yellows gradually turning to the faintest of blues. Halfway up a muddy track sunglass-wearing people were just visible ahead, most of them seeming to glow with that same mysterious half-light. The car was stuck in the mud, as were most vehicles there, so we had to walk on to the cave enclosed by the mountains as the light slowly gave form to our surround-

ings. As we passed the last of the cars I swallowed a pill from my stash, and waited to see what would happen.

There were probably a couple of hundred partygoers present, some wearing Smiley acid-face T-shirts, and the music was loud, but I had expected more people. I had been told that ecstasy made one want to dance and I danced to bring it on, and as I took another pill around a thousand people began emerging from a dark tunnel lined with local gypsies. As the crowd surged around me I was pulled down into a catacombed passageway where strangers began hugging me, relighting my joint and guiding me forward towards a faint light, which grew stronger as the space opened out.

Around me people were weaving and dancing between arches that soared above us; as the strobes spun over the cave's walls and the beats boomed them on, my body seemed almost weightless and it was as if I was merging with them, one cell of a giant being into which I was subsumed. I had read somewhere that the frequency of ecstasy-music was 140 beats per minute – the same as that of an embryonic heart rate – and in those moments it was as if I was suspended in a safe and deep womb-like space from which I never wanted to emerge again, so complete and perfect that when finally I did emerge, I was sure that it could only be as something different from what I had been before, something cleansed and reborn. Then Amber and Francesca were next to me again, laughing and dancing, and all too soon the experience began to ebb away, like the memory of a dream, as they guided me back through what now seemed a cold and blinding darkness to the car.

1

I'd never had much to do with ecstasy. Like quite a few people, I first heard of the drug at the end of the seventies, when there was talk about a new 'love pill' being used by Californian therapists to bring couples together. At around this time there was an article about it in *Newsweek*, and there were reports that Timothy Leary had married his wife Barbara after taking some, and he had predicted it would be the defining drug of the eighties. But I have to admit that I did not pay much attention to any of this talk. It seemed like just another fad in the background that was not going to be there for long. And when I had been offered it a few times at clubs in New York in the late seventies and early eighties, I'd always passed. I wasn't sure how long the effect would last, and at the time I was negotiating a complicated marijuana scam with the Gambino family, who ran JFK airport, where the produce would be arriving. I felt I needed my wits about me and, in the circumstances, it was too risky to experiment with an unknown quantity.

By the early eighties, when a gay friend took me one night to the Paradise Garage near Hudson Square, the drug was being called 'ecstasy' for the first time, not 'Adam' or 'love juice' or 'disco biscuit' or any of the other names it had been known under up to this point. Of course, at the time I didn't know this was the name that would stick. All the changes to its name made the drug feel, still, like something transient, just another passing craze rather than something that would stay around. This was at the start of the AIDS epidemic, and the club was already threatened with closure. Most gay venues were not having their licences renewed due to fear of contagion, and with all the scare-mongering at the time, I have to admit I was nervous of taking anything new. I am ashamed to say that I was rather apprehensive about being in that sort of club, and again steered clear of the little white pills when they were offered at the door.

Upstairs, the legendary Larry Levan, who I already knew from Studio 54, was on the decks, dressed as he often was like a pirate in a baggy white shirt without a collar and braces. But the scene was different. Due to the heat inside, though it was the depths of winter, the crowd were wearing light summer clothes, and though there were no spirits on sale, everyone looked spaced out in a way I had never really seen before. This was not the rhythmic swaying of dancers on cocaine and Quaaludes, the staple disco drugs at this time, but something more abandoned and trance-like. Unlike at Studio, where the focus was on socializing and getting laid, here most of the dancers did not seem to be involved in anything sexual; it was more like a collective religious merging together of some sort. A gangway made from brilliant white lights led down into this heaving throng, and my impression was of a pleasure cruiser setting out on some final and wilfully fatal voyage. The band was playing on.

My friend that night was called Ed Miles. He was known on the scene as Miles from Nowhere, one of a new generation of dealers who had grown up in the clubs, and he was just a kid, who looked like a cartoon Straw Peter with a mop of blond hair and gangling figure. All year he wore summer clothes and sunglasses in bright colours, the sort of get-up a children's entertainer might wear, but despite appearances Miles was a canny businessman. For several years he had been the pet of Susan Dee, Manhattan society's house dealer, and through Dee, Miles had got a line to Juan Royal down in Texas – the only volume ecstasy wholesaler at this time. From Royal, Miles was able to buy stock almost at cost, and with all the clubs getting closed down in New York, he was already shifting his operations to England: air-muling small amounts of ecstasy disguised as vitamin pills and distributing it into London's West End clubs, places like Limelight, Legends, Browns and Heaven.

The clientele in these places could afford to pay up to

£25 a pill, and as Miles was the only real source at the
time, he charged as much as he could get away with. He
was making about a 1,000 per cent return on his stock
from Royal – double the return he had been getting back
home. But as this was a relatively small market in com-
parison to New York, it was not long before Miles began
expanding into other cities – those with scenes which
already had networks of club dealers he could plug into
and supply – like Manchester in the north of England,
which had an active underground music scene going back
to the post-punk era.

It was not until late 1986 that I heard again from
Miles. I was back in Britain, arranging for more Thai grass
to come in by boat to Liverpool docks in a consignment
of coconut matting from Laos. The truth was I had been
missing Miles since I'd been back in Europe – his humour,
the fresh way he looked at things, and his surprising business acumen – and so I was pleased to hear from him
again. This time he was on one of his business trips to
Manchester, a place he had probably barely even heard of
while still working the Manhattan clubs, and about as far
away from that glamorous world as one could imagine.
And yet, surprisingly, he sounded excited on the phone.
'Come up and see me,' he said. 'I'm going to show you the
future.' This was a difficult invitation to turn down, so the
next night, with some misgivings, I headed over to see him
from Liverpool, where I had been staying with friends.

As Miles met me at the station and drove me down to the Hulme estate, one of the roughest neighbourhoods in the city, he kept losing his way. He wasn't used to driving on the other side of the road, and was swerving from lane to lane and crashing the gears. He had probably never learned to drive, although he had licences from several different states, all as fake as his tan. Finally he took me up towards one of the tower blocks. It looked semi-derelict, and on the way we passed a walkway with a couple of would-be muggers waiting at the other end. The youths stared, spellbound, at this strange figure in beachwear and glasses; by the time they stopped staring we had already passed them, and Miles was conducting me through a maze of unlit passages that he seemed to know his way around.

The flat at the end of this maze looked like a squat, like most of the others in the block. A couple of rooms had been knocked into a dance-floor, and I could see immediately that this was something new. The tracks on the decks were from the Paradise Garage, but now the dancers were of both sexes, and everyone was wearing baggy clothes and Converse trainers. Not much drinking was going on, and the dancing was crude and staccato, with everyone making up their own steps as they went along. This was the first time I had seen girls out dancing and not wearing any make-up, and sweating openly, and a scene where every single person in the room was grinning from ear to ear at the same time. Many were wearing those Smiley T-shirts that occasionally I'd seen on people in the New York clubs.

It seemed Miles's prediction about the future was accurate, because within only a few months this scene had already hit the over-ground Manchester clubs – most notably the Hacienda, where so much ecstasy was being consumed that no one was buying alcohol at the bar – and spread to London's gay super-club, Heaven, to the Clink on the South Bank and to the parties organized at the Ministry of Sound nightclub. These were setting the scene for such events in the future by featuring funfair rides, guest DJs and light shows as the entertainment, instead of alcohol and pulling. As the scene began to blow up over the following summer, with acid house nights in clubs like Limelight and in pubs on Portobello Road, the same cartoon look of Smiley shorts and baggy outsize beachwear I had seen that night could be seen everywhere. It was as if Miles himself had become the new normal; and seeing this reminded me how Miles had suddenly disappeared from my life at the time, leaving a void which no one else could quite fill, because Miles was a true original, though he was probably still there, somewhere in the background, orchestrating things.

By the spring and summer of 1987, there was already a lot of talk going around dealing-circles about the big money to be made in ecstasy. Friends of Miles' had begun setting up labs in the jungles of Thailand and Laos, using the established marijuana and heroin routes to reach the markets in Europe. It was through these same friends of Miles that I heard about the major summit of dealers which had been held in Barcelona in 1986. With hindsight, it was already clear which way the wind was blowing: the old ways of doing things were changing in the face of the new drug's temptations of quicker, larger and apparently safer returns. But like an ostrich, I had my head in the sand of my old ways, and at first I did not see what was coming. What started in a squat in Manchester in 1986, only three years later, through the heady second Summer of Love of 1989, had turned into the biggest clubbing scene in Europe, on a scale never witnessed before, and in 1995, as I left prison with a promise to clean up my life and go straight, fate would drop me – an ex-con who only knew the smuggling trade – into the heart of one of the most extravagant drug scenes on the planet. It would have taken Herculean willpower to resist getting mixed up in it.

Only a couple of months before my trip to Manchester with Miles in 1986, a loosely knit group of major dealers had gathered to discuss the drug on the top floor of the Hotel Majestic on the Passeig de Gràcia in Barcelona. Although I did not attend, I got an accurate account of the proceedings from others who were there. The staff that day had been told that this was a meeting of high-level plastics manufacturers, and both the penthouse suites and the roof terrace overlooking the Sagrada Família cathedral were sealed by the security contingents from the various factions and closed to the public. There had been nothing quite like this event since Lucky Luciano and the other mafia bosses had met in the Hotel Nacional in Havana three decades earlier to carve up the heroin trade, but this time everyone present was focused on the impending illegality of the methamphetamine MDMA in the United States and its consequences.

Although MDMA was at this time illegal in Canada and most of Europe, it had never been illegal in the United States, and many of those present had profited, handsomely and legally, by its manufacture and domestic distribution; none more so than the man who had called the meeting, the US national of Mexican origin known as Juan Royal. Royal was head of the Texas Group, which was already making multi-million-dollar profits from MDMA, and this was where Miles was sourcing his stock from. Its customers were able to procure the drug by calling a toll-free number and paying by credit card. Nightclubs in which Royal had a stake in Dallas, Fort Worth and Houston sold it openly over the counter. The group's production had reached almost a million pills a month, and Royal had been careful always to ensure government taxes were duly paid.

MDMA was being sold in these clubs as a dance drug,

slotting into the evolution of a new type of music emerging from the last days of gay disco: house and garage from the Chicago and New York DJs, and techno from Detroit. Neighbouring Canada had been quick to catch on, and then Europe, mainly as a result of rising British rock stars like Boy George and Marc Almond indulging themselves in the MDMA-ridden scene of Studio 54 and Paradise Garage, and bringing the news back home. As this demand had grown overseas, the Texas Group had expanded its operations by supplying MDMA to countries where consumption and possession of the drug were illegal and where buyers were prepared to pay as much as $25 a pill. This had necessitated alliances between the group and powerful criminals in Canada and Europe.

These were the men gathered around Juan Royal that evening in his Barcelona suite. Their agenda mainly comprised turf negotiations over who would control territories throughout the United States and Europe, and these had passed off largely without incident. Most of those present already had profitable local trades, and did not want to upset the status quo.

The main terms of business that had been agreed by the time the meeting ended would define the global drug trade for a generation. As the heads of the syndicates readied themselves to leave, a man called Spencer Purse, seated at the table to the right of Royal, turned to him and gestured towards the sea. Purse, a British national with a long

history of smuggling everything from South African dia-
monds to Afghan hashish, owned a series of successful
front companies: an antique and art business in London;
chemical-manufacturing plants in Switzerland, Germany
and Taiwan; plus soft drink companies in Spain and Italy.
He was a relative newcomer to MDMA, having been selling the drug for only a year, but he had already won the
respect of those present for how quickly he was developing
his turf within the Spanish club scene.

'And the Balearic Islands?' Purse asked casually, as if it
was an afterthought.

Most of the men around the table just shrugged. They
had barely heard of the Balearic Islands, which lay a hundred miles east of where they sat, and were sparsely
inhabited, apart from a few coastal resort towns popular
with Northern European tourists in the summer. They had
no significant drug market at that time, except a handful of
gypsies and hippie leftovers selling Moroccan marijuana
and acid. On the beaches were a few open-air nightclubs
where visiting DJs did sets during the summer months, and
ecstasy was consumed in small amounts, but not much else.
There was no obvious reason for anyone to be interested
in these islands, and when Purse sought the assurance of all
present that they would continue to be part of his turf,
Royal and the others agreed without hesitation.

So was struck probably the most lucrative, and conten-
tious, agreement in narco-history, as within months the

Balearic island of Ibiza would erupt into the densest consumption of MDMA the world had ever known, generating a turnover of more than fifty million dollars a year in pill sales, and making Purse's wealth and influence rival that of Royal and the original Texas Group. In the years that followed, that agreement was to have far-reaching consequences for the direction not only of the world drugs trade, but of popular culture and music throughout the world. Eventually, in the mid-nineties – by which time I would be on my way back to the Balearic island of Mallorca, only a few miles from Ibiza, and my family to rebuild my life in what had been, when I left, a sleepy outpost of the last days of the hippie age – it would also directly affect my life.

But at this point, back in the late eighties, I felt it was safer to stick to what had always worked for me, and I was still focused on importing marijuana from Thailand into the eastern United States, where the returns were known and steady. I probably made the wrong decision, because in 1988 my life as I knew it abruptly came to an end when I was busted – along with seventeen associates in seven different countries – in what turned out to be one of the biggest and most complicated DEA stings of its kind in history. Most of my time was now spent with my lawyers as I fought extradition from Spain to Florida, where I was eventually sentenced in a federal court to a twenty-five-year stretch.

During this period, I sometimes thought about Miles and wondered how he was doing, but less than I had expected; after a few months his face was already fading from my mind, and he seemed to belong to a world I might never see again. When I wrote to him, I didn't get a reply. The few times I tried phoning his production office in Laurel Canyon, where he was apparently reinventing himself as a producer, it seemed he had become too respectable and grand to take my calls, and I tried not to be bitter about that. In my heart, I wished Miles well, and settled into my new life of trying to get through the weeks and months ahead without losing my mind.

2

In the seven years I was inside, ecstasy only once intruded into my life. Although it was in a way I would not understand until much later, looking back, I can see that the direction my life would take came from what happened that day, and from the hold that event would have on me. It would be no exaggeration to say that it became the formative moment of the second half of my life, and it would forever change the lives of everyone caught up in the gravitational pull of what was to come.

I was four years into what I still thought would be a twenty-five-year stretch at the United States Federal Penitentiary of Terre Haute. One day, the guard came to my cell and told me I had an unscheduled visit, and that he would be back to collect me in ten minutes to take me to the interview room.

I wasn't expecting anyone that day; no member of the public was allowed to visit me without both my and the prison authorities' permission. I supposed it could be the local Methodist preacher; he was an accredited visitor who would occasionally pop in every few months to see those imprisoned far from home. But he had visited me less than a week earlier, and he always let me know when he intended to show up; so this left the possibility that it was a foreign cop or intelligence officer.

Although my plea agreement ruled out any obligation on my part to cooperate with United States law enforcement, it did not stop agents from other countries turning up to speak to me. Some months previously, German police had been seeking my cooperation in prosecuting alleged IRA terrorist James McCann for involvement in a Moroccan hashish deal. I wasn't very helpful. I had sworn that I had nothing to do with any Moroccan hashish deal and that as far as I knew, neither had McCann; McCann had been acquitted, despite the German prosecution taking the extraordinary step of paying the DEA agent who had arrested me to make an eleventh-hour appearance at a German court to discredit my testimony.

Finally, after much longer than the usual ten minutes, the guard returned, unlocked the cell door and led me to the warden's office. After a thorough strip search, another guard took me to the empty visiting room, and I sat down as two senior Canadian officers in the uniforms of Mounties walked in. The one who spoke was a blond man with a weak chin and watery eyes; I felt there was something odd about him, but I couldn't put my finger on what.

It seemed the officers were on a fishing expedition for information about an ecstasy dealer who had slipped their net. One of my co-defendants, Gerald Wills, was already known to the DEA as an ecstasy smuggler, so I assumed this was related to him. However, the agents explained that it had nothing to do with Wills.

'We've been tracking MDMA consignments from Europe into the east coast of the United States and Canada,' Weak Chin said. 'We believe these were master-minded by a lone-wolf operator, a major importer named Hebo.' He watched me for a reaction. Neither the name nor the scam meant anything to me, but I kept listening with a cooperative air, as if perhaps I did know this Hebo.

'Two months ago, our transponders ceased transmit-ting. Hebo and his operation appear to have dropped out of sight. There's been no further sign of him, or of the drugs. We've invested significant time and money in this investigation, and at the present time we have nothing to show for it.'

There was a short silence while both men continued to look at me expectantly. They were giving out a lot of infor-mation – more than usual – and I had no way of knowing how much of it was true. I sensed they were just doing the rounds of European smugglers, seeing what stones came loose, hoping to get lucky. They had probably spoken to a lot of others before they reached me, and covered a lot of miles. I held their stares and said nothing.

Finally, they stood up. 'If you have a change of heart, you can always contact us,' Weak Chin said as they left; but even if I had wanted to (which I definitely didn't), I couldn't have helped them.

Though I did not know it at the time, what the Canadians told me that day planted the seed of something – call it an obsession, if you like, though it always felt more deep-rooted and fundamental than that – something that would end up taking over my life entirely, and the one thing I was sure of from the start was that the Canadians would not have devoted a large budget to such an operation unless their target had been moving significant quantities of the drug.

It is no secret that a drug smuggler does not like hard work, and is usually just that type of businessman who seeks the largest return on his investment for the briefest and least amount of work. If he can achieve even greater returns with virtually no outlay at all, then clearly that will be a tempting prospect for him. This probably explains why one of the abiding fascinations, or myths, in smuggling circles is not to trade in their own drugs, but to appropriate the stash of another dealer, something larger than they could ever hope to build up themselves – something truly epic, a score that will wipe away money worries forever and bestow complete freedom and confidence on the one who controls it. This myth, one of deliverance through cunning or sheer good fortune, holds the same appeal for them as that of buried treasure for a pirate, a bank heist for an ordinary criminal, or a lottery jackpot for straight people, in that it offers the chance to make big money quickly and to do this with minimum risk or effort.

Although what the Canadians told me was already fading from my mind, and soon I would begin to forget about it as the humdrum routines of my prison life resumed, in time the Mounties' story would offer me a real-life opportunity to realize this dream. In a quiet bar by the sea, I would come across a story which appeared to offer clues as to what might have happened to that missing consignment – along with the temptation to make more money than an average person could earn in thirty lifetimes. More importantly, it would offer me the chance to do the one thing that made me feel truly alive. But that wouldn't be for a few years yet. Meanwhile, as the weeks, months and years passed in prison, I occasionally dreamed during the long hours of solitude that I might have the chance one day to make one last immense, life-changing deal – one that would set me and my family up for the rest of my life.

3

As much as possible, I followed a policy of keeping myself to myself in Terre Haute. Although I mixed with other prisoners when working in the library and using the gym and outside exercise yards, my former links with the Gambino family meant I was largely left alone by the Aryans, Hispanics and other prison gangs, and remained outside their communication networks. However, in March 1995, as the day of my release approached, it came home to me that I had little idea how the world on the outside might have changed. For some time I had closed my ears to rumours going round about drug deals on the outside, and I had been keeping away from any trouble that could lengthen my sentence. Most of what one heard inside was unreliable in any case – some of it wishful thinking, some deliberate misinformation, and most just plain old wrong, repeated around the place like Chinese whispers. My experience was that nothing good ever came from listening to it or taking it too seriously. But all this isolation had come at a cost.

My access to the media during this entire period had been severely limited. The only television I had seen was in the black-gang-dominated dayroom, but this was always tuned to the hip-hop channel, and men in baggy shell suits and gold chains did not tell one much about the world beyond their own. The radio stations that I could just about hear in my cell offered no news broadcasts and instead churned out a variety of country music, which I have had trouble listening to ever since. The few news-papers I had come into contact with over the years were local ones, and the people mentioned in them had increas-ingly meant nothing to me; my letters were often rationed, and when people wrote to me, they never filled me in on what was happening out in the wider world. If you had asked me in the days before my release to stake my life on whether the queen was still on the throne, or who the current president was, I probably would not have taken that bet.

I wondered how I would cope out in the real world, as I had no money and no profession to fall back on, and it was almost thirty years since I'd had any sort of straight job. Once upon a time they had called me the largest dope smuggler in the world, the man who controlled a fifth of the world's hashish and marijuana traffic – probably something of an exaggeration, but it had provided an iden-tity I had never argued with, and in those years I had always felt I was living the life I wanted to, and that I knew who I was. But who was I now? Probably no more, in the cold light of day, than a half-remembered name from the tabloids, a name from the past; and after so much time inside, I had begun to lose sight of the confident, self-assured person I had been when first imprisoned. During this time, every cell in my body had changed, and mentally I was no longer the same person at all; the simple truth was that I was probably not going to find out who this new person was until I got back into the world.

It's a strange thing, but what long-term prisoners yearn for most is probably not freedom itself, but the moments just beforehand when all the dreams you've had inside are still intact, nothing has disappointed yet and every-thing still seems possible; and certainly, in those first hours and days after my release, I saw nothing that clearly pointed the way my life should now take.

On the flight back to the UK I ordered several bottles of red wine, as had been my habit in the old days. I was not expecting to remain a free man for long: the cabin crew had already told me my temporary passport was being withheld, and I was sure that I would be re-arrested on my arrival at Gatwick. There was nothing stopping Scotland Yard charging me on evidence that had not already been used to convict me. In '81 I had been tried for importing several tons of hashish to Scotland, but the case had collapsed after dubious testimony that I was an agent of the Mexican government; it was known I had paid the Mexican official to give evidence at the trial. A senior officer, the head of the Thames Valley Police, had committed suicide in the chaotic aftermath – something they were unlikely to have forgiven or forgotten.

But fortunately, and much to my surprise, there were no police waiting when the door of the plane opened or in the arrivals terminal. Maybe the US authorities had not given the right flight information, or not bothered to notify Gatwick in time, or more likely the police had just gone to the wrong gate, as it had apparently been changed at the last minute. So as quickly as I could, looking over my shoulder all the time, I bought a British Visitors' Passport, valid for one year, at Gatwick airport's post office, using a four-year-old book about me, *Hunting Marco Polo* by former *Sunday Times* Insight reporters Paul Eddy and Sara Walden, as identification. In the book were photographs of myself from the eighties in various disguises, taken from my false passports at the time. Somewhat bizarrely, the lady behind the counter accepted these as proof of my identity, without a birth certificate, driving licence or other corroborating ID. I booked myself onto the next flight out to Palma, Mallorca.

I felt I'd had a narrow escape. My wife and our three children were waiting at Palma airport, not certain whether I would make it through. They drove me to our house in La Vileta, where they were still living despite various attempts to confiscate it by the DEA. Although the police in Britain almost certainly knew where I had gone – and I was now in contravention of the terms of my release from federal custody, which had stipulated that I remain on probation in the UK – I was no longer worried. As extradition arrest warrants from Britain to Spain had only come into effect the previous year, it was not at all a straightforward procedure, and the Spanish authorities could be expected to be far from cooperative. I felt I would be relatively safe as long as I remained in Spain and did nothing to come to the attention of the authorities – which was exactly what I intended to do.

At that point, I could not see beyond resuming the family life that had been cut short, and did not want to see beyond it: I was in heaven, the children were mobbing me, and we could not get enough of each other. I had thought I would never know joy again, but now I did and it was overpowering. The happiness in those first days was so intense that I constantly felt close to tears. My wife also seemed genuinely happy to be with me again, and though there was a little awkwardness after so long, which was only natural, I was confident it would pass.

A few days later I was also reunited with my parents, who had flown out from Wales. Both were in frail health, and had been holding out until the time of my release to see me one last time. So many times I had cursed myself inside for visiting worry upon them in their old age, and prayed that they would be able to forgive me, as they had already stood by me, and supported me through thick and thin. I felt I owed them so much. But there were no reproaches, and both seemed overwhelmed to see me and stressed that I should not blame myself for anything, though of course I did. As my father had been a highly decorated Merchant Navy convoy commodore during the Second World War, he was no stranger to smuggling, and he told me I had done nothing to be ashamed of. They kept reminding me that I was still relatively young, and that I should focus on making a fresh start.

This was a time of immense relief for me. Inside me there had always been the lurking fear that I would not be forgiven. Now I felt myself being buoyed up by the love from all sides, and my senses were coming alive again. For so long I had been living an endless winter of solitary confinement blocks and half-subterranean cells, not seeing the sun for months at a time; my view had been other walls, or the block of death-row where they were building a new lethal injection execution chamber. Just to look out of the window now and see the sunlight over the grass felt like a privilege, and gave me hope. The simple food my wife and daughters cooked – pasta, stews, paella – tasted extra-ordinary, like manna from heaven, and just to smell it mingling with the fresh air through the patio windows seemed the greatest luxury. I hoped it would never end, but of course I knew it would.

4

The first signs that all was not well with my wife were subtle ones. At first, I think, she wanted to make sure I bonded with the children again, and did not want to risk spoiling the homecoming. We had been together for nearly three decades, and had shared almost everything during that time, so I took her loyalty for granted in the way one takes one's right arm or one's sight for granted. She felt part of me. But this shared history also had the effect of blinding me to how she might have changed. In hindsight, I should have thought more about what she had been through – about her own period of imprisonment, entirely undeserved, that had separated her from the children, and how this might have affected her – but my thoughts were always elsewhere, with the children, and daydreaming in the sunlight.

Almost eight years, of course, was a long time for a husband and wife to be apart, and she confessed early on that she had been unfaithful, which did not exactly come as a surprise. Who could blame her? She had not expected

I would ever be released, at least not before I was an old man. She had felt alone and vulnerable, and I could understand only too well why she had done it, but male jealousy is a strange worm, and I found I could not ignore what had happened, even though I wanted to, and the knowledge of her infidelities had put a flaw-line through something precious.

The marriages of long-term inmates do not tend to fare well, and it seemed mine was going to be no exception; all the banalities of such situations soon began to apply to us, and though at first we had tried not to admit it to ourselves, there seemed little I could do to stop her stating what was now obvious to both of us. She told me we had grown apart, and after so long I was no longer the man she had once known. I seemed a stranger to her now. Part of me knew she was right, as I had become something of a stranger to myself.

So, predictably enough, I began finding more and more excuses to get out of the house, and on one of these first trips out alone I went looking for a certain bar in the old town near Plaza Gomila called Chotis. It was a place where smugglers and career criminals of various sorts met – faces, as they were known – and it had often been in my mind while I was inside. I had promised myself a drink or two there when I was released, and many times I had imagined the moment of my entering; there would be a moment's hush, then maybe a few old-timers would clap and raise their glasses, and I would know I had come home.

I was fit after all my exercising inside; I had been pacing several miles a day, and working in the gym. I had noticed that I kept losing my balance and feeling dizzy whenever I passed a busy street, but I put it down to the uneven camber of the old lanes; something I was not used to after only flat surfaces and steps for so many years. I had heard of other prisoners having such problems so it didn't worry me too much at first, but with all this attention on my balance problems, I passed the bar several times without recognizing it. The place looked as if it was under new management; the booths that had once been a hub of gossip and deal-making were all empty, the comforting semi-tropical decor of the old days had been replaced by neon Buddhas and beads; the young, bearded barman, a new fixture also, was wearing a lot more of those around his neck, and at the back I recognized only one face.

This was, predictably enough, Mick Niall, once the main fixture of the place in its heyday and a big-league pot smuggler, who now looked as if he'd fallen on hard times. His laces were undone, his clothes crumpled and he had a beaten-up air about him. I wondered what had happened to him, but was too polite to ask directly, as Niall was a criminal of the old school and his pride had always been important to him. He was the sort who would never let anyone down, whatever the cost to himself; whose code had been don't grass, don't rip off, stand by your own and never back down. During my years of imprisonment, he had been one of the few friends and associates who regularly checked my kids weren't starving. He was about the last person I would have wanted to see in this state, though I was happy to see one of the faces from the old days.

My immediate instinct was to try to find out what was wrong and help him – but of course I had no money to lend, and before I even asked, he kept assuring me that he was fine. In fact, once we got talking, he seemed more interested in helping *me* out, and it struck me that perhaps I was projecting as desperate an air as he was. Eventually, the subject came round to my immediate prospects.

'If you're looking to get back into the game,' he said, with a glance at me that suggested I looked as if I was, 'now's the time to do it. When they least expect it.'

I wasn't sure what to say to this. Inside, I had spent many hours imagining what I might do if I was free. Sometimes, in rare moments of exaltation, I had of course fantasized that I would smuggle the biggest load of the finest dope the world had ever seen; but mostly I had promised all that was holy that if my prayers for liberty were answered, I would go completely straight and never break the law again.

'I don't know,' I replied slowly. 'I'm still thinking about what I might do next.' He gave me a sceptical look, as if it was only a matter of time before I went back to my old ways. As if to illustrate his point, he ordered a double Irish whiskey and put it down in front of me with a satisfied expression. As he watched me drink, he told me he had a flat in the nearby neighbourhood of Santa Ponsa that he wasn't using. He passed me a key.

'Use it any way you need to,' he said. 'It's registered under a company name, untraceable. You could use it for a bit of business, if you want. Or a bit of pleasure!' He winked. I wondered what strings, if any, came with accepting; but I took the key a little hesitantly, and put it in my pocket. Niall seemed to relax slightly.

'Been in touch with any of your old contacts yet?' he asked, a little too casually. There it was; he had been building up to this. I shook my head.

'Most of them turned informers at my trial,' I reminded him. 'I'm on my own now.'

He nodded. 'How about Malik in Pakistan, Phil in Bangkok?' These were major traffickers who had agreed to testify against me, but in the end didn't need to as I pleaded guilty.

'I'm not sure it's a good idea to contact them again,' I said carefully. Niall then began filling me in on a scam involving some contacts from Jamaica working at the airport and the docks. He was looking for buyers in Europe, and he stressed the magnitude of the opportunity, but it all felt a little unreal to me. He kept stumbling over his words;

the details kept sliding about and changing, as if he was just talking the talk, reliving his glory days when maybe he couldn't deliver anymore. I reminded him that Malik and Phil were exporters, not importers, and so would be of no use in his scam in any case.

Niall looked crestfallen at this, but seemed to accept it. He fiddled with his glass and asked in a more subdued tone, 'Have you spoken to Old John?'

'I called him.'

'How did he sound?'

I shook my head. 'Weak.' Old John, my former partner, was one of the few who had not betrayed me. As Niall already seemed to know, Old John had advanced pleural mesothelioma, a cancer of the lining of the lungs. In over twenty years he had only once had a straight job – when a teenager, he had been an electrician for two years – and during those two years, asbestos dust had invaded his lungs. Now, over thirty years later, it was asphyxiating him.

Hoping to pierce Niall's gloom, I offered to contact some of Old John's people on his behalf and see if they would do business with him. I reminded him of Old John's man in India, the legendary hippie Seagoon, whose Nepalese and Menali had been the best dope you could get. But at this, Niall shook his head and looked even more dejected. 'Nobody wants the good stuff these days, the quality hashish,' he said, in a tone that implied this was something we both already knew. 'It's all about hydro-ponic skunk, and cheap Moroccan soap bar.'

It seemed the world had changed more than I realized. Here we were, two ex-cons completely at odds with the modern world, which in just a few short years had left me far behind. I had not been harbouring imminent plans to scam again, but it was becoming clear that the door to my old trade was closed whether I liked it or not. I had always smuggled quality Thai, Pakistani and Himalayan, and I had no contacts in these newer markets.

From what Niall said, this change had been determined by simple market forces. Instead of taking the frightening risks of international smuggling, better returns could be secured by gardening skunk locally. As for the Moroccan dominance, half of Europe's criminals lived in Spain's Costa del Sol, across the water from the main production fields, and as the routes were short and well-established this was a low-risk, quick-return game. This Moroccan gear was cheap, consistent, and everyone knew what they were getting; but like fast food, it was soulless and empty. However bad things got, I knew I could never bring myself to deal in it. There was no romance in that business, which was a large part of what it was about being a dope dealer across three continents that had given me such a buzz for all those years. Though I had not smoked dope or tobacco for many years, the Moroccan I had taken the day of my release had not even got me stoned. I hoped that whatever

I ended up in, it was not selling Moroccan soap bar, as I knew I could not live with myself if I fell to that.

By the time Niall left me alone in the bar – now almost empty, which it had never been in the old days – a depression was beginning to settle over me. I called by a couple of clubs in the area, hoping for some distraction, but it was a wet, miserable winter evening and no one I knew was there. When I called some of the old numbers of friends on the island, no one was at home; or if they were, they were not answering my calls or they had changed their numbers; or maybe it was a combination of all these things, but I could not find anyone to join me, and so my mood only darkened.

The clubs around the bar were full of a younger crowd than had been the case a few years ago, and they had changed beyond recognition. In the old days they'd been typical Eighties pulling palaces with their tropical decor of plastic coconut palms and glitter balls, populated by scantily dressed girls from the mainland on the prowl for rich men to look after them. Now I wasn't even sure if these were the same places. It seemed the prediction Ed Miles had made was accurate, as most now resembled giant versions of the dive he had shown me in Hulme. All the kids inside were wearing baggy clothes, smiling a lot and not drinking alcohol, and I guessed they were all doing ecstasy. There seemed little obvious distinction between the boys and the girls, at least not in the low strobe lights, and there was no sign of the sort of girls in sleek tight clothes who had lit up the floor in the old days. Now everyone was dancing all the time as one heaving, sweating mass, and these girls wore no make-up and looked as if they hadn't washed for several days. I felt nothing at all when I looked at them and wondered what that said about the state I was sliding into.

My immediate problems in those first months were mainly financial. Though there had been reports in the press since my release that I had stashed away millions in Eastern European banks, I was in reality stone broke. Money-laundering had not become an offence in Spain until '95, but all my Spanish accounts had been used up over the years on legal fees, and the dozen other accounts I had kept for a rainy day in Switzerland, Sicily, Hong Kong and Thailand had all been tracked down by the DEA and local drug agencies during my incarceration and sequestered. Several million dollars had disappeared without any proper audit or due process being followed, even though most of it had been earned legitimately by my former travel and secretarial businesses, and there was little chance of ever getting the money back, as I did not have the funds to hire lawyers, and I had run out of favours that I could call in.

When an offer came through to me from the well-known publicist Max Clifford, to sell my story to the

News of the World for £10,000, this helped in the short term; but though I had no objection to doing business with Clifford, whom I had always found pleasant enough in previous encounters, this sort of money was not going to last long. Bills for the house were piling up, as builders and other local businesses had been patiently waiting for my return. I also had debts to Balliol College, who had lent me money while inside to finance my daughters' school fees.

Selling more stories to other papers for a few hundred pounds helped me scrape by for another few weeks, along with writing some book reviews. When a friend from the old days, Lynn Barber, approached me to do an interview for the *Telegraph* I wanted to charge her, but knew I wouldn't get away with it. As Lynn was one of the few people I had known before I went into dealing and smuggling – she had briefly been a girlfriend of mine – I hoped she might be useful in finding employment in the journalistic world, and I spent a lot of time trying to remember our past together as a way of getting back into her good books. But all that was coming back to me were the basic outlines: how we had met at the Kemp cafe, a student hangout, when Lynn had been the girlfriend of a leading student actor, Richard Durden-Smith. After he left her for another starring student actor, Maria Aitken, Lynn, by her own account, had gone on the rampage, and I had been part of her rampage. To be fair, it had been the Sixties, and we had been stoned all the time, and a lot of girls were on

the rampage. Lynn's theory that you should have sex first
to see if you were compatible, not waste time on courting
that ended in a damp squib, must have paid off, as she'd
met her husband, David Cardiff, while she was doing the
rounds of the male campus, and they had been happily
married for thirty years. During this time she had built up
a reputation for well-observed psychological insights on
her interviewees, finding out their less well-defended weak
spots and hitting the mark; so I dreaded reading her piece
about me, but most of it, thankfully, turned out to be
harmless reminiscence and I felt I had been let off lightly.

With Lynn unable to help me on the career front, and
the money from the papers running out, while I was still
living at the family house in La Vileta I reluctantly drifted
into a little dealing to friends in the neighbourhood to keep
my head above water, but this was kept deliberately low-
volume; it was strictly a stopgap to generate money to
survive on until I decided what to do. But it meant I now
had daily contact with small-time suppliers in Palma: Mick
Niall and other former smugglers who, like me, had fallen
on hard times. In an echo of the old days of waiting around
for deals to go through, I spent hours of frustration searching for empty telephone kiosks of the right type, which
took something other than credit cards.

Of course, I did not have a credit card, and if I did get
through I'd be led through several expensive diversions to
an answering machine; and so as I trudged around the

hillsides getting soaked, the idea of buying a mobile phone – which was still a novelty, and was going to set me back considerably – became increasingly tempting. The last time I'd owned one it had needed a car to power it, preferably a BMW or Mercedes or a battery box the size of five kilos of hashish, and it had worked on radio waves, meaning it was a piece of piss to intercept, and had furnished evidence used against me at my federal trial in Florida. I felt I probably knew how to use mobiles more prudently now, and finally, against my better judgement, I drove to a phone shop and bought a non-account, top-up phone which could be used anonymously. I used the phone as sparingly as I could and left it switched off as much as possible. I made sure it was off as I approached the family house, never made calls off the local mast in La Vileta, and varied call points as much as I could. If the cops were monitoring Niall's phone and putting tags on any numbers that called him, they could not easily predict where my number was going to phone from and make a collar – at least, that was how I rationalized it. I had learned many things while in prison, and I was not going to get caught out again so early by the new technology, which I was only just beginning to understand.

I had also started smoking copious amounts of dope again. My routine was to keep straight during the daytime when I was doing my few local deals, and not dip into my own supply until after seven every evening. To avoid tobacco, which I had given up while inside, I resorted to consuming the cannabis in cookies – but there was something rather non-macho about passing around a cookie, however cosmic, and the more stoned I got eating them, the more I found I missed the sensation of smoke in my mouth. After bongs, vaporizers, hot knives and inverted glasses were all put through their paces, finally the inevitable happened and I succumbed to a tobacco joint. I had been out of prison for only a few months, and I was now fully reacquainted with the old Howard Marks. Aside from the obvious disappointment of having already broken the promises that I had made to myself and my family, it did feel good to be back. I was finally feeling like I had rediscovered myself, that I was human again.

This lapse only seemed to open the floodgates, and all the resolutions I had made about clean living and starting over began falling away. Within days I was also drinking alcohol again, and it wasn't much longer before I was combining joints and booze, and waking up in the mornings in a bad way, thinking I was back in my cell, or with no idea where I was. Some mornings, there was so much sweat on the sheets they had to go straight into the washing machine. Sometimes I was not convinced I had woken up at all, and I couldn't go back to sleep because I kept thinking I already was.

During this bad patch the rest of the family were increasingly avoiding coming into my room, and I was spending most of my time getting stoned, and paranoid, alone in the apartment Mick Niall had left for my use in Santa Ponsa. This behaviour felt a rational enough reaction to the bad news which had been piling up around me all that year. After years of fighting a series of chronic illnesses in order to survive until my release, my father had died in the early spring a few weeks after his visit to me on the island. Old John, who had been another sort of father to me, had also finally passed away from his lung disease in the summer. Soon after this, Niall, who had been supplying my dealing, had been robbed and badly beaten up in London and had developed a serious heart problem. One by one, my old contacts had been getting in touch with more miserable tales of former colleagues who had died or were doing long prison stretches, so when I received the news that Niall had suffered a fatal heart attack, I could only wonder where the axe would fall next and what form the next piece of bad luck would take. This was not at all how I had imagined things would be on my return home.

5

Given that most of my old contacts had agreed to give testimony at my trial – and that their phones were almost certainly bugged – I had probably been unwise to talk to any of them so soon after my release. I had hoped they might at least provide me with leads into some sort of regular income, but I was to be disappointed, as all said they were no longer smuggling and most said they were broke. They were now into small-time laundering, buying items in cash – usually motorcycles or cars – then coming back the next day for a refund, and asking for it to be paid into a bank account. They tried to get me involved, but it was a messy business: half the time the retailer wouldn't take the item back, or only at a big discount, and the item would have to be sold on for less. Before you knew it, only two-thirds of the investors' money was being returned, which caused ructions. A bent bank or currency shop would take smugglers' cash at less than a 10 per cent fee, so this was for mugs. Sure enough, two friends of Niall's were busted within weeks of my hearing from them and sent on remand to La Modelo in Barcelona, where a prisoner could wait years before his case was heard. This seemed like a warning to keep my nose clean.

It was around this time, in the late summer of 1995, that I was paid a visit by Gordon Walker. It seemed innocuous at the time, but I would later look back on it as the first in a sequence of related events. Walker was a larger-scale money-launderer than the others; we had become close while we were both in the top-security Centro Penitenciario Álcala Meco prison, in Madrid in '88, while I was awaiting extradition to the US. It was a prison reserved for ETA members serving the maximum sentences allowed by Spanish law, and for those who had committed very serious offences while serving time at other Spanish prisons. It was also the home of those fighting high-profile extraditions, such as Jorge Ochoa, leader of the Medellin Cartel, Pizza Connection boss Gaetano Badalamenti, and me. All of our cells were solitary confinement, and I never saw any other type. But as the only two British nationals, Gordon and I had been allowed limited association time during the hour or so of exercise permitted each day.

Although we had become friends during these months when he had been fighting extradition to Britain for his involvement in money-laundering, I had not heard from Gordon since, and at first I didn't read much into his visit to my house in Palma. Indeed, he told me it was just a social call to welcome me home, and he had brought along an envelope of cash – a typical old-school gangster tradition of welcoming someone to freedom. I was relieved to have some cash in my pocket, and more than willingly invited him for drinks by the pool.

Of course, like half the island, I was aware that Walker had been one of the main launderers of proceeds from the 1983 Brink's-Mat heist, the largest gold heist in modern criminal history. Twenty-six million pounds' worth of gold had taken over a decade to launder through almost every conceivable kind of asset – including ecstasy – and this had been a bloody business. Everyone knew that Brink's-Mat had been the cause of most of the killings in the underworld for more than a decade. Throughout the 1990s it was the defining event to which every criminal act in Britain and mainland Europe seemed to be linked.

On a bitterly cold night in November '83, a gang of Bermondsey hardmen had broken into a secure unit on a trading estate near Heathrow. They had expected to find three million pounds in cash, but they had stumbled into what would turn out to be the largest heist for over a generation: they had found not cash, but over £26 million in pure gold ingots, and probably the same amount in jewellery and other precious metals. It was the equivalent of a haul of over £75 million in today's money. Most had been owned by City banking firms like Johnson Matthey, so the massive scale of the haul could be estimated from the insurance claims. It was a sensational robbery, the likes of which had not been seen since the Great Train Robbery of 1963. It fed the red-top newspapers for years to come as the police tried to piece together what had happened and went about tracking down the gang.

Over the next fifteen years, over a dozen killings were associated with the heist. The basic problem was that the gang had no experience with gold, so the converting of the gold into usable assets had to be outsourced. This was a slow and tricky operation – not least because as the network of those involved widened, so unfamiliar names crept into the operation, not all of whom could be trusted. Turf battles ended up being fought between members of the gang over control of the various hiding places for the caches, as well as over the laundering. One of the smelters was a Welshman I knew, an associate of Walker's. The network had spread so wide that even the former Great Train Robber Charlie Wilson had become mixed up in the recriminations as various factions of the gangs fought for control. Several of the killings had recently been covered in the newspapers, and the fallout was still ongoing when I was released twelve years after the robbery. It all served to make me a little wary about the real purpose of Walker's visit.

When a gangster makes a social call there is almost always another reason for his coming, but that day Walker left without giving any clue as to what this might be. While we talked about the good times he seemed relaxed. He told me he had several deals going on, without getting into the details. He had the air of a successful property developer, smoking and gesturing with a big cigar. Throughout the afternoon he kept getting up to make calls some distance from the house, presumably to get updates on the deals: this was a courtesy of sorts because if his calls were being monitored, as they probably were, they would not be tri- angulated back to my residence, and I would not be associated with them.

Everything remained at the level of small talk: if any hints were dropped as to the real purpose of the meeting, I did not pick up on them. By that point, the Brink's-Mat fallout felt like something very far away in which it was difficult to imagine myself being caught up; but now, with hindsight, I can see that Walker was probably assessing my suitability for something. I suspect that this was at the heart of all the strange events that followed; but this is one of several things about that time that I will probably never know for sure.

I was distracted by other events as well. After the *News of the World* interview earlier that year, I had been approached to write an autobiography by the editor Geoff Mulligan from the publishers Secker and Warburg. The payment of the advance for the book meant I no longer had to dabble in small-time dealing, and it covered my immediate debts and my living costs while writing – but doing so swallowed all of my time for the next six months. Fortunately, one of the first things I'd done with my second week's takings from the neighbourhood dealing was to buy a computer. It was complicated: mice, Windows, scanners, CDs gumming up the works – all this was new. Still, parts of the keyboard looked vaguely familiar, and I spent the mornings pecking away, hoping to stir up some latent creativity. The family still left me alone in my room during these sessions, knowing better than to interrupt me when I was smoking, but it felt like I was gradually pulling myself up again through the writing from the low point I'd been in. That my drawers were full of press cuttings made the writing easier, as did copies of previous books written about my life, such as *High Time* and *Hunting Marco Polo*, which I'd used as my identity at the airport. But – like all serious dope smugglers – I'd kept no diaries. I had also been stoned for much, if not all, of the period concerned, and could not remember the years or even the order in which my scams had taken place.

Luckily, a solution presented itself in the form of a letter from my United States defence attorney, Stephen Bronis, who wanted to know what he should do with a pallet full of what Americans refer to as 'discovery' and the British as 'depositions' – the documents of prosecution evidence against me. Air-freighting these across the Atlantic cost me £2,000, but it meant I had copies of the investigations concerning my activities compiled by the law-enforcement authorities of fourteen different countries; meticulous surveillance reports of my daily life carried out by the DEA; cassettes of dozens of hours of taped phone calls; and transcripts of debriefings of co-defendants and grasses.

Although I might not remember where I had been at any particular time, I now had the means to determine this with precision. Over the following months, I began to piece together exactly what had happened over those years. It is, ironically, thanks to the American legal system that I was able to launch my second career as a writer. Without its meticulous recording of my life, I would never have been able to reconstruct the events that led to my incarceration.

The book, however, raised a new problem: even before it was published, I would have to spend time in Britain to raise my profile, and then I would be needed again later to promote it and to do readings and signings. I had already slipped back in a couple of times for funerals by using one-way tickets bought at the last minute (which meant the authorities had less time to act on the passenger list manifest), but this was an expensive way to fly. I knew it was only a matter of time before my luck ran out.

Sure enough, on my very next arrival in Gatwick in October '95, the police were waiting – several uniformed border officers, along with three of Scotland Yard's finest. Though I tried my best not to be intimidated, in reality I was. One of the three looked as if he wanted to give me a beating, and another talked of locking me up again and throwing away the key. He said this as if he meant it, and suddenly all those memories of being extradited out of Spain and languishing in foul-smelling prisons for months on end came rushing back to me. I had no desire to repeat that experience.

Facing them in that small interview room, not knowing what they could do to me, I remembered an old joke one of my Spanish cellmates had told me while we awaited extradition all those years ago: in a perfect world, all the cooking would be done by a Frenchman, the clothes would be designed by an Italian, the appliances by a German, the length of the holidays decided by a Spaniard . . . and the policeman would be British. I doubted he would have held to that view if he had seen the looks these three were giving me across the table.

There was nothing, in theory, to prevent them from charging me with major smuggling and money-laundering offences on the basis of evidence that had not already been used against me in my trial in Florida; or with similar offences, but under British law. There were no UK statutes of limitations on such offences, so the defences of pleading *autrefois acquit*, *autrefois convict* or double jeopardy did not apply, unless the evidence needed to prove the charges in the separate jurisdictions was identical. Thankfully, after several tense hours, they seemed content to tell me that they did not consider it in the public interest to prosecute me after so long. 'But step out of line again, and you'll know about it,' one of them added. It seemed, in the end, that they just wanted to rattle the cage to warn me. I left the interview room in dire need of a joint.

Still feeling shaky, on the trip into London from the airport I noticed that when I went through the busy terminals and concourses, my stomach began churning and I felt dizzy and nauseous. This was similar to what I had experienced in the crowded lanes of Palma's old town. At first I had put it down to unfamiliarity with walking on uneven surfaces; but now it was happening in perfectly flat spaces, and it seemed to be triggered in some way by being among crowds of people. I realized that what I had probably been experiencing was 'cell shock', a condition that affects long-term prisoners. It commonly presents as agoraphobia, fear of crowds and stage fright. It was as if my nervous system had grown unaccustomed to the open, populated spaces of the outside world. As long as I was indoors, or away from crowded places, I was not affected, but here in the city, constantly surrounded by people, and increasingly estranged from my family, it was easily triggered.

On arriving at the hotel I had a double brandy, but this just made things worse. Even when I went outside and smoked a large joint, which would normally have settled my nerves, the feeling of panic persisted. I realized that I might experience problems presenting a poetry reading the following week, *The Return of the Reforgotten* at the Albert Hall featuring Allen Ginsberg and Paul McCartney. I had read widely while in prison – one of the few pleasures that we were encouraged to pursue – and this event was part of the reason I had returned from Spain. It was also an early step towards giving me a higher media profile in the run-up to my book being published the following year. But now, feeling as frail as I did, and knowing the event would be a crowded one, I feared the worst.

Sure enough, on the night of the reading – just a few minutes before it was due to start, as I was looking out at the crowd from behind the stage curtain – I was hit by another dizzy spell, my most severe yet. Ten years later, I suffered a bout of cardiac arrhythmia, and was prescribed beta-blockers to slow my heart down and relieve anxiety. The effect was similar, but I felt more out of control this time.

I could see another smoker over by the door; he had the pallid, drawn look of someone on regular medication, and I reckoned he probably had something on him that might help. I approached him, but he shook his head, gesturing with his unlit cigarette at a group of mellow-looking youths sitting on the steps. 'There you go.' He caught the eye of one particular youth, who returned the look enquiringly. '*That's* who you need to speak to.'

The boy in question turned out to be called Hatter.

He and his friends were wearing home-made robes and
hats – they were probably students from the fashion college
next door – and he was selling something he said would
work like a tranquillizer. Normally I preferred to know
exactly who I was buying from, and what I was buying,
but in the circumstances I felt I had to take a chance. By
the time I was on the stage I felt calmer, with a warm,
selfless energy pulsing through me. I was able to make the
introductions to a packed house without the least flicker
of nerves. Exactly what I had just ingested, I was not
sure.

The card Hatter gave me showed he lived in Soho, not
far from my room at the Groucho Club. This was just as
well, because my diary for the next few months was full.
At each of the events I attended around London – many
of which were crowded and stressful – I made sure I had
his wraps with me; often I accompanied them with cocaine
to provide energy, as the clubs in Soho were awash with
the stuff at this time and it was difficult to avoid it. But
about half an hour after each line I would feel edgy again,
most unlike I was accustomed to from hashish; however
much I smoked, it did little to lessen my anxiety, and this
only increased my need for the pills.

I was so preoccupied with this wonder drug that I did
not really notice how London had changed since I had
been away. It was apparent that much of the Eighties
confidence had disappeared. During the last ten years

there had been many changes: the City had gone through the Big Bang and Black Wednesday, house prices had boomed and then crashed. As we headed towards the final year of John Major's Tory government, the streets looked dirtier than I remembered. The city had a feeling of uncertainty and transition about it. The news was still full of the fallout from the Barings Bank collapse and the Nick Leeson scandal, and the war in Bosnia rumbled on; the people on the streets I glimpsed out of the corner of my eye looked dowdier and more anxious than in the old days, their faces as preoccupied as my own. It felt as if something was about to change, but what exactly wasn't yet clear.

I was now in daily contact with Hatter. I tried to find out from him what exactly the pills were, so I could find an alternative source for emergencies, but he was rather vague, just calling them 'easy boys'. All it took was a quick call and in half an hour he would leave more at a certain bar on Dean Street, or meet me there. By the spring of '96 I was getting high on my own most days, staying indoors as much as possible. In the build-up to that summer's Euro 96 football tournament, I found myself supporting Spain until they were knocked out by England in the quarter-finals, when I reluctantly shifted my support to the home side. When I went out for any length of time, to give readings or watch matches at friends' houses, I dropped a pill and took a line in advance. This pattern continued into the autumn months, when the launch of my book meant I was in higher demand than ever.

All the time, the comedowns were getting worse. Nothing mitigated the feelings of exhaustion and desolation except taking more pills, and I began hoarding them along with wraps of cocaine. At any one time I had half a dozen wraps and bags stashed around my room, so that in the event of a bust I reckoned on at least one of each remaining to me. Unsurprisingly, it was not long before Hatter could no longer keep up with this level of consumption: often he was delivering less than was ordered, and his quality was becoming inconsistent, so that soon I had no choice but to look for a more reliable dealer.

Some regulars in the Groucho Club recommended I seek out a man called Nicholas Saunders – not as a dealer per se, but as a connection to the best and most reliable West End dealers around at the time. With Saunders, I was to get rather more than I bargained for. Not only could he source produce of almost any sort and of the very highest purity, but it seemed he was also a figure at the heart of the underground ecstasy scene; a scene of which, at this point in 1996, I was still barely aware. His name was already known to me in connection with the popular *Alternative London* publications and the Neal's Yard health-food empire, both of which he had founded and of which he remained sole owner. The rumours I heard about him sounded far-fetched: it was said he had his own purity testing laboratory, and travelled around in a special van with an on-board lab, and that various European governments sent pills to him for analysis. Later, I would learn that all these rumours were true.

I first met Saunders in person on BBC's *Newsnight* when I was being interviewed by the host, Jeremy Paxman, as an advocate of marijuana legalization. Saunders was on to talk about ecstasy. It was a role he already seemed familiar with, and he spoke a lot about how the drug cauterized man's destructive impulses and elevated his selfless and loving nature. He seemed to see it as something which had the potential to bring peace and harmony to the world, as nothing else had. He sounded more like someone on a divine mission than a drug dealer, and he seemed strangely serene, like some sort of monk.

Afterwards, in the green room, he laid a fold of pure MDMA powder on me and a dozen pills. 'A gift for you,' he said with a smile. 'I'm not interested in making a profit; I'm a facilitator, if you like. A guarantor of purity.'

This meeting was brief, no more than a few minutes; but he had made an impression on me, and in the phone calls which followed it felt as if we had known each other all our lives. It was the first time since I had come out of prison that I found I had properly connected with someone on the same wavelength as me. From the beginning, Nicholas Saunders was someone I felt at home with and instinctively trusted, and I recognized that this encounter marked a major turning point in my life. But whether this would be a change for good or bad was not something I could call yet.

6

Having spent the rest of 1996 on tour with my book, I returned to Mallorca for a holiday. I didn't exactly feel refreshed – the gruelling schedule of signings and talks, along with the drugs, had seen to that – but I did feel as if I had my mojo back, and it was not long before I was on the plane back to London.

In January '97 I was invited to DJ at the ICA with two friends: Anita Pallenberg and Johnny Edgecombe, who was Christine Keeler's ex-partner. It was a roaring success, although I had never done anything like it before. I was enjoying my new status as a celebrity author, and I was promptly booked for more sessions. I was also asked to write a regular column for *Loaded* magazine by the editor James Brown, and was selected to run in the May general election, in four seats, as candidate for the Legalise Cannabis Alliance. The *Independent on Sunday* invited me to head a legalization rally from Hyde Park to Trafalgar Square. Most weeks, my name was in the papers in relation to these activities. I would be lying if I said that I didn't enjoy my rekindled notoriety, and the attention from the fans that came with it.

Probably, with some patience and effort, I could have consolidated and developed all this into some sort of steady career in the media. Instead, increasingly I was leading what could only be called a double life. I still thought about the thrill I'd felt when I'd carried drugs through the airport on New Year's Eve. Most of my nights were now being spent with Nicholas Saunders at ecstasy raves to which he brought a portable laboratory in his van, parked outside venues like the Fridge in Brixton or the Clink on the South Bank. Our favourite haunts were the underground warehouse spaces where raves were being held since the Criminal Justice and Public Order Act of 1994 had targeted any gatherings with music characterized by 'a succession of repetitive beats'. Unlike the mainstream licensed West End clubs of the time like Heaven, Limelight, Legends or Ministry of Sound, these raves tended to be one-offs for which the address could only be obtained at the last minute by calling a number printed on the event flyers. Ecstasy had been making the news for the wrong reasons with a number of highly publicized deaths, and Nicholas offered a free service for testing clubbers' pills in a converted suite in the back of his van. A drop of Marquis reagent was added to evaluate purity, and micrometre readings of the pill's dimensions and their scoring were compared with charts of existing products from German-

and Dutch-held databases. This service was publicized at Green Party Drugs Group events in Brixton, and if the clubbers' pills were not good, the real thing was for sale from approved dealers who were at hand to take care of them. Most nights these dealers could clear upwards of ten grand from this operation, of which we were given a generous cut to cover the costs of the van.

Now that the market was growing, potential earnings from the drug were at an all-time high. The smaller labs tried to brand and differentiate their own product in the marketplace and the pills came in every shape, colour and size; each time a new pill became popular, cheaper adulterated copies would flood the market within weeks. The copies were often cut with amphetamines and potentially toxic solvents and benzoates, so this testing process outside the club had become essential to anyone wanting the genuine ecstasy experience. The testing was the brainchild of two of Saunders' colleagues, Dennis Watkins and Elisabeth Dermot, who also happened to be former associates of mine from my dope-smuggling days. The couple were old-school hippie refugees from San Francisco's Bay Area who had washed up, like many others of their kind, on Britain's South Coast in the early seventies. They had stayed on to deal dope and acid and now, predictably enough, had diversified into the drug of the moment – ecstasy.

I felt it was probably safe to be around these two characters, as neither had been caught up in my trial and both had solid reputations. This apparent trustworthiness was reinforced by their still having that familiar early-Seventies look of long, straight hair and collarless shirts. In poor light, which was usually the light one saw them in, both still reminded me of Mike Oldfield at the time he recorded *Tubular Bells*. In another age this look might have seemed gauche, but it was becoming fashionable again. Dennis and Elisabeth had come back into their own, and when kids came up to them in the clubs and asked where they got their threads, they were chuffed to bits.

I had known Elisabeth for almost thirty years, since we had both been postgraduates at Sussex University, and we had gone out briefly. At that time Sussex had been a centre of the counterculture, known as Balliol-on-Sea. Elisabeth did not look anything like a dealer; she looked clean-cut, wore a lot of Jesus jewellery and went around in a battered old wagon with born-again bumper stickers. This was a look she had perfected over the years, to the point that it had become part of who she was. It had become so convincing that I was no longer sure how much was just front, and how much her real self. Some of the innocence of that earlier time still ran in her blood now, overlaid with the hard-headed business sense which had helped her to survive in a man's game for so long. Although I did not know Watkins so well, he was cut from the same cloth, an old-school Sussex figure who had adapted to the new market. We had friends in common in Mallorca, where he and

Elisabeth both owned property. I felt he was probably trustworthy to be around, as he came with Elisabeth's endorsement.

The pair's ongoing project was importing a large quantity of pure MDMA by boat to the eastern seaboard of Canada, where wholesale prices had held up well in the face of cheap Asian imports and were almost on a par with the US. Although returns of 700 per cent were being dangled, I hesitated before getting involved. The memory of how real I had felt on New Year's Eve at Palma airport several months previously was still there when I closed my eyes, but so was the hollow laughter that had followed. While it was clear that Elisabeth and Dennis only wanted me to act as a consultant on the logistical side of the operation, I continued to hesitate, even though they were calling me every day.

By early June – a few weeks after Tony Blair's landslide victory in the General Election, soundtracked by D:Ream's 'Things Can Only Get Better' – the news was still full of pictures of Alan McGee and Noel Gallagher meeting Blair at Number Ten. Elisabeth and Dennis gave me an ultimatum: either they heard from me within seven days, or I was out. I was still tangled up in indecision, and when the week passed without my getting in touch with them, I felt a sense of relief that I had kept out of it.

But then, rather to my surprise, a few days later they let me know that there was a delay to their project over

the summer, and they gave me another more flexible ultimatum. This time, I had three months to make up my mind
and arrange some of my old contacts as buyers. It was
clear from Dennis and Elisabeth's messages that my inabil-
ity to give them a timely decision previously had caused
them to miss deadlines. I felt guilty over this, and I did not
want a reputation for being unreliable. After much agoniz-
ing, I just dipped a toe in the water and provided them
with two shipping contacts in Montreal and a small
amount of investment. But small as it was, there was no
doubt that it reminded me of the thrill of the game. Such
is the dilemma of the ex-con: I was so determined to go
straight, to turn over a new leaf, but at the same time
keenly aware that this was who I was, and that this was
what had defined me throughout my adult life.

As the summer of 1997 drew to a close, sales of the
paperback of my book were reaching 1,000 copies per day,
thanks to a strong marketing campaign on the Underground by the publishers. It should have been a good time
for me, but my friendship with Saunders was beginning to
take its toll. I had now been using ecstasy almost every
night since before the election and throughout the summer,
when the rave season reached its zenith. I was also reliant
on the prescription sleepers and sedatives, Clonazepam
and Halcyon, which I was importing for my personal use
from a pharmacy in Valletta in Malta. I had been attending
weekly rave nights at the Fridge and the Clink, Sunday

nights at the Milk Bar and most weekend warehouse parties within the M25 area, along with raves in Manchester and Bristol when I had been there promoting my book. While I still had a strong constitution, I was not a young man anymore, and my body could no longer spring back into shape automatically as it once had. In fact, my body and nervous system felt close to breaking point, and while I still felt the buzz, I was desperate for some sort of exit strategy. Although I was aware I had not been home for over six months, since the new year, I felt in no state to go back and face the reality that my marriage no longer existed, and therefore no longer offered a shelter, until I had cleaned up and felt stronger in myself.

7

When the German publisher of my autobiography invited me to stay with him at the end of that summer, I felt it was the opportunity I had been waiting for. I stashed all my pills in a locker in a branch of Mail Boxes Etc. in Notting Hill Gate and set out, clean, for the airport. I wandered about WH Smith and the other shops in an anxious daze. It had already occurred to me that the German authorities might have unfinished business with me. In '78 I had left the country in a hurry and abandoned a stash of money in a safety deposit box, registered under the name of Donald Nice. It was likely they had found it by now and traced it back to me, as this alias had been exposed at my trial. In addition, a load of Lebanese hashish that I had sent into the country a few years later had also been intercepted, and it was possible there were warrants still out for me over this. When the German cops had visited me in prison in the US, I had been far from cooperative and had provided them with far from accurate information. They might well have been holding a grudge, which they would now be able to act on.

But in the event there was no problem with immigration at Frankfurt airport – though if I thought I could take a breather in Germany I was to be disappointed, as my German editor, Marcus, turned out to be a hippie with dreadlocks and was clearly in the mood to party. No sooner had I landed than he began rolling a joint in plain sight of the cops and promising harder action to come. As the car filled with smoke he told me we were heading first to Heidelberg, which I had expressed an interest in visiting. Within seconds of listening to him talk, it was already apparent that I was in the company of a stoned but highly intelligent conspiracy theorist – always a dangerous combination, in my experience.

By the time we entered Heidelberg city limits, Marcus had already confided that the war on drugs was in his opinion all due to the Nazis. He explained that the Nazis' main problem had been being unable to discover a drug that turned individuals into unthinking and aggressive murderers, as every drug just seemed to turn people on or chill them out. In his opinion, the only partial exceptions were American cigarettes and cheap lager. This conspiratorial chatter started the moment we left the airport, and by the time we reached Heidelberg my head was aching.

As soon as we arrived in the city Marcus launched into a new conspiracy theory. It seemed that Heidelberg had been the centre of the booze and tobacco industries in Germany for several centuries; this, Marcus believed, was why the Americans had taken over the city's tobacco factory, Landfried House, after World War Two. It happened to be next to the railway station, and they cut off the excellent Turkish and local tobacco supplies and got the Germans hooked on inferior Virginian product. At this point I suggested that in that case it was just as well we, the Brits, had got rid of the Nazis – at which Marcus looked rather offended and told me that in fact the British had themselves been Nazis from the start, right from the top. England and Scotland's first king was James Stuart, and his daughter, Elizabeth Stuart, had come to Heidelberg and married the German king, Frederick V. Since then, it was his view that the British ruling class had always been crypto-Nazis, and controlled by Nazis, and this had been consolidated by the House of Hanover. Even Queen Victoria had been educated at Heidelberg, ensuring she was indoctrinated with Nazi ideology from the start.

By this time we were both quite stoned, but it seemed Marcus's definition of Nazi was rather an elastic one, as he went on to assert that they were still very much in charge. But instead of coming from Heidelberg, they came from further west, as Heidelberg now served as headquarters for the US Seventh Army, the Central Army Group and the Fourth Tactical Air Force. When I asked why we had fought those wars against each other, if we were in fact all

Nazis and on the same side all the time, Marcus explained that this was to 'get rid of our arseholes, Howard, every country has them', and that 'the only point to wars is that they cull such arseholes'. As much as I liked Marcus, it was clear that the less time I spent with him, the better it would be for my mental wellbeing.

Marcus's patter finally ebbed away as we parked outside Heidelberg castle and entered the German Pharmacy Museum. The displays immediately drew me in. There were prescription counters, bowls for blood-letting and medicine chests. In the next room glass cabinets were crammed with thousands of brain-tickling chemicals: friendly plant stuff like opium, morphine and hash, unfriendly plant stuff like curare, a South American arrowhead poison, and powdered toads, ground lizards, and organs of human mummies. Further in was an Aladdin's cave of distillation heads, glass retorts, crucibles, stone ball weights, powder mixers, pill machines, tab dividers, pastille presses and pewter enema syringes. Of course, seeing all this only made me think of Saunders back at his lab, and Elisabeth and Watkins waiting on our consignment on its way to Montreal. My anxiety, which was already unpleasantly sharp, only increased.

The labels said these last items had all been donated by the pharmaceutical giant Merck AG of Darmstadt, which Marcus told me was our next destination, where he lived, and also where ecstasy had been invented eighty years ago. At this point I went silent. The way Marcus told it, during the sixteenth century the founder of the Merck company, Friedrich Jacobs Merck, had been born and bred in a place called Schweinfurt, which he referred to as 'Pig Castle'. According to Marcus, he had been such a dedicated worshipper of drugs that he set up a dope-manufacturing company called Angel Pharmacy, which he housed in Darmstadt, the City of Entrails. The company had been owned by the Merck family ever since, and by the 1900s it had more than 1,000 employees. After the war, when the Americans took charge, within a month the company began manufacturing dope again. It was impossible to get any sense of whether any of this was true or not.

Now Merck had over 20,000 product lines, production facilities in over twenty countries and a further 170 companies operating worldwide on its behalf. But the official statistics failed to mention that its pharmacists had first synthesized ecstasy two years before the First World War, in attempts to find an effective anti-blood clotting agent, and a patent for manufacturing the compound had been granted two years later. Whether true or not, it felt like a typical stoner's story.

On entering the town, Marcus told me we were going directly to a rave venue where the ecstasy on sale was made by young chemists from the Merck factory in their spare time, and that it was some of the finest gear available. I had hoped to go clean while I was in Germany, but on hearing this all my good intentions went out of the window, and I tingled with an almost erotic anticipation. I could always dry out when I got home, I reasoned with myself. I was still in this state as we reached the Krone building, where the event was held. It was one of the few in Darmstadt to have remained intact since the war. Marcus ushered me quickly through the hushed chill-out room, and from there into thickening crowds in a yard below where there were several small stages, stalls and a large marquee called a panzer tent.

Inside, on a platform, was a full-size tank and what appeared to be a small spaceship. When I touched the side of the tank, expecting it to be made of plastic or fibre-glass, it was cold metal. Marcus explained that it was 'a reminder of our past, and how best to deal with it these days'. Now I saw that it was named 'Think', and inside were decks and DJs. The spaceship next to it, Marcus told me, was a V2, an unmanned rocket-bomb of the sort aimed at London during the war and pioneered in Darmstadt by a certain Werner von Braun, who had gone to the States to work for NASA – who in turn had set up the European Space Agency, the control room of all Europe's satellites, in Darmstadt. According to Marcus, 'the city liked dicks': the first space rocket had been conceived of there, and it was the testing site of every condom sold or exported from Germany. This place, which I had barely heard of, was now feeling increasingly like the centre of the world.

My head was aching – as much from Marcus's craziness as the dope he had given me – so we went into the
bar, a quieter space with gentle Eno-like music. I chewed
the capsule Marcus had passed me. It tasted bitter, with a
lingering aftertaste, and my first awareness of anything
strange was an overwhelming urge to expel my false teeth
from my mouth. I wanted to spit them out onto the floor.
My lower jaw felt fragile and began shaking, and I could
not drink my beer. For reasons I still don't understand, I
took off my watch and left it on the bar.

Back on the stage, the DJ inside the tank was letting
loose tidal waves of hard-core techno, and all around it –
including on its roof – beautiful human bodies were
dancing. Suddenly the tank seemed to be communicating
with me directly across the crowded floor, telling me it had
had a miserable life, witnessed immeasurable suffering,
death and sadness, been stuck in trenches, overturned in
bloody mud, shot at, impounded and abandoned – and
now it was born again. A new smoke filled its lungs, joy
boomed from its veins, and huge, gracefully drifting psy-
chedelic images glided across its surface. So this was what
pure ecstasy was like. In all my years of drug-taking, I had
never experienced anything quite like this.

In the far corners of the chamber, red globe lights
glowed. Spaceship balloons descended on us, silver confetti drenching the dancers, green lasers piercing the clouds
of dry ice. As the intensity and frequency of the flashing

lights increased, so did the beats per minute of the music. The beats seemed to be emanating out of my body, and my skin was becoming clammy and sensitive to the slightest vibration. I felt completely surrounded and overwhelmed by the rhythm, the fruit-flavoured smoke preventing me from seeing more than a foot ahead. As I reached the edge of the space, the windows seemed to have become mirrors and the floor was ceaselessly undulating beneath me, the strobes transforming the dancers into frozen, jagged shapes, something alien and unreachable.

Marcus's voice penetrated the noise. 'Just dance,' he shouted into my ear. 'And drink this. Keep dancing and drinking, and it will get better.' He pressed a bottle of Lucozade into my hand. I danced and I drank; but it didn't get better after all, and we stumbled back outside. When I switched on my phone, I could see even through the drug haze that the news was not good.

There were messages from Elisabeth Dermot and Dennis Watkins saying my name was all over the Spanish newspapers in relation to the Montreal scam. Although the details were confused and inaccurate, it was evident that the cat was now out of the bag. Some of the articles stated I had been involved in a very recent large importation of hashish into Montreal, others that it was club drugs; but all mentioned Montreal, and the approximate route the consignment had taken. Though the Spanish authorities were on record as saying they were not interested in proceeding against me, Dennis and Elisabeth had, worryingly, both also been named, and the authorities had given no undertakings that they would not be coming after them.

Still swimming through my comedown while Marcus administered Lucozade and other support, I tried to get hold of them. They weren't answering their phones, but I was told they were in Spain, in Mallorca, and their apartments there had already been turned over by the local police. My contacts said that they had headed to the relative anonymity of the Costa del Sol, down in the south of Spain, well away from the heat. The next day – after I was contacted by several journalists, including one from the *Sunday Times*, and asked to comment on the Spanish reports – leaving a message for my family on the answerphone at the house in La Vileta saying I would have to be out of touch for a while, I decided to follow suit and lie low.

8

Although I did not know it at the time, moving to Spain in late 1997 was to prove one of the defining moments of the second half of my life. It was either the most fortunate or the most unfortunate thing that could have happened to me, depending on how one looked at it.

I felt it would be wise to avoid travelling through London, in case the interest of the *Sunday Times* and other English journalists rolled over into English police interest in the matter. Thanking Marcus for his hospitality in Germany, I got a connecting flight via Mallorca to Malaga on the Costa de Sol. I travelled on my own documents because they were all I had with me. Old friends were arranging a place for me to stay at short notice. They were associates of Gordon Walker, the Brink's-Mat money-launderer, who I had contacted mainly because they were unconnected with everything that had just happened.

The place was a golf chalet near the seaside resort of Estepona, about ten kilometres west of the larger resort town of Marbella. This southernmost coast of Spain, hanging down like an untucked shirt below the rest of the country, only a few miles across the Straits of Gibraltar from North Africa, was a busy holiday destination in the summer but now, out of season, it was quiet. The chalet was in a particularly remote location; around it there were just a few slumbering retirement communities and run-down holiday villa complexes, most of them already closed down for the winter. Over the next few weeks, everything in my life would appear to slow down considerably.

My friend's place, which was normally used only for a few weeks in the summer, felt as if it hadn't been lived in for a while. It smelt heavily of mould. I couldn't find keys to any of the windows to air the rooms, and the place needed a good clean, but I wasn't complaining. It was nicely low-key, and it was warm enough most days to sit outside.

My plan now was to keep my head down and do some writing. With *Mr Nice* well-established, I harboured hopes of a new life in letters. In the mornings I sat with my computer on the terrace, looking out at the foothills of the Sierra Blanca, the range of hills inland from the coast. The rest of my time was spent exploring the overgrown golf course and the paths down to the beach.

It was good to have a moment to reflect. I had spent the last year promoting my book, talking about the past, about who I had been, what I had done; but I hadn't spent much time thinking about who I was now. Some people might have been happy to perpetually relive the past, but I needed more. What I'd realized, writing my auto-biography, talking about it to so many people, was that smuggling had been about more than just the money. It was about setting myself against a system, and beating it. I'd eagerly embraced taking ecstasy and found something extraordinary happening there, but I couldn't escape the suspicion that much of it was at least partly to fill the emptiness of days with nothing else to fill them. If I wasn't a smuggler, then what was I?

Even for an ex-con, paradise can get boring. Each day now felt like an eternity, and stretched ahead of me without the prospect of much happening. In truth, I missed the action, as well as life away from the children, who I had not seen as much as I had hoped to now that they were grown up and had their own lives. I also missed my marriage as it had been in the old days, though I was now resigned to that time being passed forever. Wandering a little further each afternoon, I saw hardly anyone along the way. Further down, nearer the sea, there was a sort of ghost town of empty summer apartments and shuttered-up bars, and some strange sunken tennis courts, about half the normal size. These had fallen into ruin. Nearby was a bar which had all the appearance of being closed, its shutters down, *cerrado* on its door; but sometimes it opened for a few hours in the afternoons. On the walls were pictures of long-forgotten stars of *padel*, the game whose courts I had passed. The barman told me the sport had once rivalled tennis in popularity, but due to its arcane rules had gradually gone into decline. Now only a few courts remained.

Behind the bar were some warped old rackets shaped like beach bats, and in one corner were heaped ancient copies of the various English-language papers: *Sur in English*, *Aloha*, *Marbella Life* and the like. For lack of anything better to do, I would leaf through them while I sipped my drink. Mostly it was just local gossip and pieces syndicated from better-known publications, but one afternoon something caught my eye. It was an article about a local drug dealer who had fallen off a three-storey building, but the details were rather sketchy. The man had apparently been a recent arrival on the coast. His real name was not known, and the article ended only by saying there were rumours that the man had taken the location of a large consignment of ecstasy to his grave.

Perhaps I was looking for something to occupy me, but I was struck by this story, and kept turning it over in my mind. It was only about an hour later, as I wandered home, that I remembered the story the Canadian Mounties had told me back in Terre Haute, about the missing dealer. Undoubtedly there was some resemblance between the two stories. The next afternoon, I went back to the bar and saw that the article was dated about two months before the Canadians had called on me – about the same time that they said they had lost sight of their mark. I knew this wasn't conclusive; still, when I retreated to the chalet and tried to concentrate on my writing, I found my mind kept returning to what I'd just learned. A strange idea was taking hold of me, and would not let me go.

When I called the English-language magazine where the piece had appeared, they said the writer was no longer working for them, and they had no forwarding details. A few calls, and more enquiries about him, turned up nothing. This didn't really surprise me; that coast around Marbella was a fly-by-night sort of place, and people moved on all the time.

The next day I went to the nearest public library, where upstairs there were stacks with all the local and national newspapers, and spent an afternoon going through all the publications of the same period. There was nothing in the nationals, and the local papers carried only some one-paragraph reports of a man falling off a building in the New Golden Mile. This was an area about five miles along the coast from the chalet, to the west of Marbella. Various construction projects out there had run into financial problems, and most of the condominiums and holiday apartments were still empty. In the report, the man was described only as an American passport-holder; there was no mention of him being a dealer, and no more details were given.

Hoping that she might be able to fill in the picture, I called Elisabeth Dermot and arranged to meet with her the next day in a bar in Estepona Port, about fifteen minutes down the coastal highway. The Montreal deal had ended badly, the consignment had been lost when it had apparently been intercepted by Canadian authorities on the St Lawrence river, and so no one was seeing any return on their investment money, but as yet no one had been pulled. I did not want her to come to the house or the local bar by the ruined courts, because if the police or anyone else checked later, they were likely to get a description of anyone seen with me. I wasn't sure if there was still heat on her over the Spanish newspaper reports about the Montreal scam – if so, it was heat I didn't want to pick up. The bar I chose was not overlooked, and it was situated on the busy frontage of the port, so we wouldn't attract attention.

As usual, Elisabeth arrived looking nothing like a dealer, wearing her Jesus jewellery and driving her battered old wagon with born-again stickers which she had driven down from Mallorca. The years had been kinder to her than to the rest of us. We cut to the chase, and within only a couple of minutes of talking, she had given me a name.

'Oh, that was Henry Bowen,' she said immediately on hearing my description of the story. 'He was American. From the Bay Area.' At first this meant nothing to me, and

I kept Elisabeth talking for an hour or so, hoping to turn up more. It transpired that she had only met Bowen once in a crowded club. 'He was friendly with Nicholas,' she explained. I was slightly apprehensive about sharing too many details about why I wanted to find out more, and left it at that with Elisabeth, but we promised to stay in touch.

I felt confident Nicholas Saunders would know some things, and that he would talk to me. I phoned him straight off from the nearest payphone, but was told he was away in South Africa. I left a message asking him to get in touch as a matter of urgency.

Four days later, I still hadn't heard back from him. When, finally, I tried his number again, his long-term part-ner told me he had been killed in a car accident on the third of February – three days previously, the day after I had spoken to Elisabeth. His partner seemed surprised I did not know already; his car had apparently run off the road for no obvious reason. It was a new hire car, and the road wasn't dangerous, but the chances were that Saun-ders was driving high at the time, and post-prison paranoia aside, I knew it would be a mistake to make too much of the timing of this.

Saunders was someone I had been close to, and I felt he had been unambiguously a force for good in the world; so the news struck me hard. It was at this point that things started to go a bit weird. I called Elisabeth Dermot and

Dennis Watkins to see if they had more details of what had happened, but neither of them got back to me. This was a little unusual, and I learned from mutual friends that neither Elisabeth nor Dennis had been seen for several days. They had not been returning anyone's calls.

There were potentially many innocent explanations for this, of course; but that night, just to be on the safe side, I left the chalet and checked into a nearby motel, the sort where one could put a bank card in a machine which issued a key-fob, with no one at reception to notice who came and went. Every few hours, I did some passes of the chalet in the car to see if anyone was watching the place; but as usual, there was no one else around, and the surrounding streets looked deserted. Thinking I was probably worrying unduly, I left my car a block away and crept back in, and for the next few days I kept the lights off and stayed out of sight at the back. Not wanting to leave a smoke trail, I ate my dope rather than smoking, but this only made me more edgy. I wasn't even sure what I had got myself into, and perhaps it was age catching up with me; but I had a definite suspicion that by asking too many questions, and through simple association, I was courting a kind of danger that I had never experienced as a dope smuggler.

The chances still were, of course, that Elisabeth and Dennis not getting back to me was unrelated to what was happening. People like that ducked out of sight all the time and for all sorts of reasons. But every day without word from them felt a little more ominous, and so over the next week I began trawling the criminal hangouts along the coast, hoping I would run into them or get word of them. All the while, I quietly went about trying to gather more information on Henry Bowen. My thinking was that if someone did not like questions being asked about Bowen, this behaviour might trigger a reaction from them and make them show themselves – though my expectation was still that there was an innocent explanation for what had been happening. Whether I was paranoid or not, a picture was starting to emerge that did more than just connect the dots.

As the days passed without anything bad happening, I began to relax a little. I became something of a regular in the bars where I was making enquiries and kept to more or less the same routine every day, so that if anyone had information for me, they would know where to find me. Most mornings I called at Sharkey's, a favourite gossip hole a few miles down the coast. It was probably one of the most charmless bars in the world, sitting as it did next to a sewage outlet from the nearby hotels on a strip of imported grey shingle which had been washed away by the flow. The place had to be approached across a series of perilous duckboards; these passed a storage hangar for jet-skis, the type often used to tow in drug consignments from bigger boats on the straits, and the group of younger runners who worked them could usually be found in the bar with some older faces. I never learned anything of value there.

The rest of my day was spent shuttling between the Terrasana restaurant, in a ritzy area west of Marbella known as Nueva Andalucia, and certain bars down in Puerto Banus opposite, where most of the local big shots kept their yachts. The names and decor of these places had changed over the years, but the clientele of retired and semi-retired criminals who frequented them seemed to have remained the same. The trail ended at Dreamers nightclub, where some of the same big shots had private tables, or at Key Boite in the Puente Romano Hotel, which in the jet-set days had been the upmarket Regine's, but was now another run-down escort joint. This half-mile strip, which housed the Saudi villas and the swankier golf clubs, was where everyone on the coast tended to congregate at night. Most of the people I wanted to talk to could usually be found either in these two clubs or at the larger clubs, La Notte and Olivia's, which catered to punters from the straight world. But no one had any word of Elisabeth or Dennis. Though people were reluctant to talk about Henry Bowen, it seemed that he was stale news; everyone trotted out the same basic story, but when you came down to it, no one really seemed to know much.

After several weeks, I had learned only that Bowen had appeared on the coast out of nowhere and booked himself into a three-grand-a-night chalet at the Marbella Hill Club Hotel. One night he had got drunk and sounded off about a major consignment he had bound for the States; then, a week later, he had fallen off a three-storey building behind Cancelada on the New Golden Mile.

There seemed no doubt that what had happened was a genuine accident, rather than foul play. Bowen had gone in to view an apartment off-plan, and lost his footing. Twenty builders down in the yard having their lunch break had been witness to his being alone in the building at the time. The man had no local friends or associates that anyone knew about, nor had he been seen trying to make new contacts on the coast, and another week of doing the rounds brought me no new information about him. Working bars as far afield as Sotogrande and Malaga brought no new information, either; it seemed the Bowen story had become set in stone, and no one had anything to add.

But I couldn't curb my instinct to keep searching for answers. Finally, in desperation, I turned to some old contacts in the Policía Nacional, despite knowing that it would cost me and that the information wasn't always reliable. As winter moved into spring 1998, I was close to the point of giving up and was not really expecting much to come of this, but it was the only avenue left to try. And sure enough, in the end, one of them got tired of my pestering and gave me something.

9

At this point, I should probably have known better than to continue, and called it a day. If it's true that you can know a man by his friends, then Henry Bowen's association with Pierre Antar did not show him in a particularly good light.

Antar's name had come to me from a certain Policía Nacional official who I had once paid off in relation to a dope scam in Mallorca. The official was known to work a lot with grasses and informers. Whether this was how Antar had got onto his radar was not clear, but what I did know was that Antar was a Moroccan heroin user with a reputation for being untrustworthy and, worse, slippery. His habit had eaten up his trust fund and he had a bad reputation for setting up big deals, demanding a lot of samples, and then disappearing. He was probably not above selling information to the police if he got into a tight corner. He was easily bored, and was known for causing trouble just to pass the time of day. In short, the first mention of Antar's name should have set alarm bells ringing.

My contact told me that Antar had gone to ground because he owed people money: nobody was sure where he was. The only tip anyone could offer for finding him was to go through a former society dealer, a friend of Antar's and an Englishman called Mark Hadley who was now based nearby. I already knew Hadley a little from the old days, when he had sold smack to rich kids in Notting Hill and Kensington in the eighties. After a couple of his clients had overdosed he had started over in Spain, organizing free raves and yoga retreats in the hills around Granada. For most of my life our worlds had not collided, and he was the type of person I usually avoided. He lived in a bungalow in El Paraiso, a run-down urbanization in San Pedro de Alcántara, only about five miles east of my chalet along the coastal highway. On the phone he seemed surprised to hear from me, but when I told him what I was after, he sounded cooperative.

When we met, Hadley was almost unrecognizable behind all the long hair and hippie gear. Almost a decade on, it seemed he had still not lost the spirit of the Summer of Love – or at least he wanted it to look that way. The first thing he told me was how ecstasy was going to bring peace to the world. It might have been Saunders talking; but the difference was, I didn't think Hadley believed a word he was saying. Despite his hippie look, there was still a faint air of menace about him.

When I enquired about Antar, Hadley appeared willing

to help without naming a price or asking anything in return. Against my better judgement, I took this at face value; I hoped it was a sign that he had really changed, though I couldn't ignore the fact that some of the stories I'd heard about him were troubling. Usually, when a smack dealer's clients died, he would take the blame whatever the circumstances. Most dealers live under some kind of cloud for the rest of their lives if they are implicated in an accidental death. But sometimes dealers can emerge from these tragedies as better human beings – as Hadley seemed to be doing. While no one in Spain seemed to know about his past, and it was never mentioned by either of us, the shadow of it hung between us whenever we met.

I vaguely recalled that there had been a run of society heroin deaths at around the time Hadley got unlucky. Olivia Channon, a Tory minister's daughter who had died in 1986, was perhaps the best-known; and one of the Tennant boys, Lord Glenconner's sons, had overdosed and been hospitalized in the same year, probably on Hadley's gear. After Joshua Macmillan had died a few rooms away from me in our Oxford days, heroin was a world I had always kept away from; Hadley had only come onto my radar because he was part of the group around Robert Fraser, an art dealer who was a friend of a lot of rock stars. Fraser knew everyone hip on the gallery scene, and he was an old friend of mine and an old friend of practically everyone's; but this was later when Fraser had come back from India with a beard and a heroin habit, and moved in different circles. It worried me a little that I couldn't remember Hadley more clearly from that time, because it made him more of an unknown quantity now than I would have liked.

Indeed, Hadley had always had a reputation for being someone whose name you heard quite a bit but you rarely saw in person. He always seemed to be in the background of things. The only definite memory of him that I could dredge up came from one night in the early eighties, when I had stopped for a few minutes at the Tennants' house off Campden Hill Square to pick up a friend.

It was a large, rambling place within which various members of the family had flats. The Tennants owned the island of Mustique and were millionaires many times over, but the house was squalid; most of the light bulbs were out, and one had to feel one's way down a long passage before coming into the light. I could vividly recall that the rubbish had not been taken out, and there were maggots crawling around the floor. Charles Tennant was sitting on a chaise longue with some friends, smacked out of their minds and babbling like children. All the while an old lady, perhaps in her nineties, was sitting in a corner asleep. Hadley was standing in the same corner, looking entirely sober. He seemed a bit embarrassed when he saw me, and said he was just leaving.

Not once in the course of our discussion about Henry

Bowen did Hadley make any reference to this, or anything else from the old days. It was as if we had never met before. Later on he suggested that we go out, and as we drove around he tried to interest me in various business schemes he had going on. One involved a black box which he plugged into the cigar socket. 'It emits ozone particles,' he said. 'It'll clear the toxins from any enclosed space. Here, I can smell the smoke on you – that'll be gone in minutes.' He switched it on, but I couldn't tell much difference. He had another contraption that went over the head ('It massages your sacral planes. Try it!') and did nothing but give me a mild headache. A further black box, which supposedly realigned all chakras if placed on the chest, was equally unconvincing; when I shook it, it made a sound like dried peas rattling around.

Eventually I managed to steer the conversation back to Pierre Antar, who seemed like the most obvious lead in the search for Henry Bowen's stash. I had known Antar only a little before his habit had taken over, but he was one of those people who you would see around at clubs and parties, usually hidden away in a dark corner. I doubted Antar would mislead me about Bowen, unless there was some entertainment to be gained by doing so. Hadley explained that he was taking me to an apartment in the old-money neighbourhood of Guadalmina Baja, where he said he'd last seen Antar.

When we pulled up, we found the flat locked up and

covered in bank repossession notices. It was clear that no one had been there for a very long time. The next location we tried, a holiday apartment complex in Banus, he had only stopped at for a few days; but we did manage to get some sketchy directions to a cabin in the national park above Gaucín in the Serranía de Ronda. At this point Hadley became visibly nervous, and began to make his excuses. Before long, he had peeled off, and it took me almost another full day to find the place.

It was up in rugged country which had once sheltered the old smuggling routes up from the Campo de Gibraltar and was home now to dense, recently planted cork forests and the nesting grounds of migrant African birds. The March sky hung low over the trees that obscured views ahead. The cabin turned out to be a half-subterranean structure, almost entirely hidden by the forest canopy. During that year the authorities were still patrolling the skies, looking for illegal buildings, and it had been con-structed to escape notice from above. On one side were some abandoned vegetable runs and on the other, under camouflage netting, an ancient Toyota Land Cruiser. No sooner had I stopped than a figure ran out at me from the trees, gesticulating wildly.

Antar was a foot shorter than me, but he had the advantage of surprise, and I only just made it back into the car. 'You dog!' I could hear him shouting, along with other words in Arabic, all of which sounded like curses. He was scraping at my door with a blade – an antique, by the look of it – but I didn't think he intended to do me any real harm, just to frighten me. As it was a rental, I was not concerned about the car, and just kept the window closed until I had worked out what was going on.

It came back to me that I'd once – long before my incarceration – had a disagreement with Antar in a night-club called Joe's in Puerto Banus. He clearly recognized me, even though more than ten years had passed. It was a trivial matter which I had forgotten about, and after I apologized profusely, he settled down and invited me into the cabin.

Inside there were no signs of any drug paraphernalia, and I wondered whether Antar had hidden himself away in such definitive isolation to get clean, or whether he was just very keen not to be found. Books in Arabic and a variety of other languages were lined up neatly on make-shift shelves, along with pictures of Antar as a youth on the streets of Tangiers with an older man who looked rather like William Burroughs. Whatever the reason for being here, it was clear that Antar had made himself at home. He invited me into a relatively clean kitchen and offered me some stale pitta spread with oil, and mint tea – the sort of thing one would get at a Moroccan workers' cafe. It looked like I wasn't the only former drug smuggler in these parts who had fallen on hard times.

As we reminisced about our respective good and bad

fortunes, Antar's voice sounded shaky. He looked to me as if he had been through a lot, and nothing much would surprise him; as if he was old before his time, and just wanted to retreat from everything and rest. I waited for as long as I could before I brought up Henry Bowen, but when I did, Antar just rolled his eyes.

'You know, half the faces on the coast were chasing after that stash of his once he was gone. A lot of chancers, too.' Antar shook his head and drained his tea. 'Same day the news broke that he was gone, some idiots from that jet-ski hangar turned his place over. Found nothing. Just a bag of pills and a bunch of keys.'

'Keys to what?'

'Nobody knew, so they necked the pills and just drove around wasted, trying to open everything everywhere. Turned out, they were for a couple of golf lockers in Nueva Andalucia.' Antar grinned. 'One set of clubs in there. No drugs.'

A few days later, Spencer Purse, the man who ran Ibiza and one of the most established names on the ecstasy business, had sent down some of his own boys to do a more thorough job. They had paid off the staff at the hotel and reconstructed Bowen's movements to try and trace where he had spent his last hours. This was no small feat, given the legendary discretion of the hotel. They had also gone through Bowen's computer and phone records before the police had managed to get hold of them, looking for payments linked to storage facilities; but nothing had come up.

'How do you know all this?' I asked Antar.

'I was one of the guys Purse paid.' He shrugged. 'Happy to help. Not that anything came of it.'

What I found interesting was not that their efforts had proved fruitless – I had expected as much – but that Bowen, a low-life foreigner with no apparent connections to the island, had come to the attention of someone like Spencer Purse. Purse was an international businessman, running over a dozen companies worldwide from private banks to soft drinks conglomerates; too big an operator to waste resources on some open-ended treasure hunt. Either Bowen's stash was something epic, or there were other, more sinister reasons why Purse wanted to clear up Bowen's affairs. However, according to Antar, Bowen had never worked for Purse, which echoed what I had already heard. By all accounts Bowen was a lone wolf: not only a smuggler, but a lab man, someone who knew how to make the drug to a high level of purity. This meant that the chances of tracking his consignment from the supply end were next to non-existent. Most likely, Bowen had just cooked the batches alone in a bush lab, then voided the place.

I had recorded the conversation with Antar, and I listened to it again several times over the following weeks. He still spoke with the drawl of a posh boy, not finishing his sentences, barely starting them before he seemed to lose interest, but one got the drift soon enough. During those weeks we spent quite a bit of time together up at his place, and he showed me the trails through the cork forest. The bark was harvested every five years, and the rest of the time the forest was deserted. I got the feeling that Antar didn't often have visitors and was happy to play tour guide in his little world. I felt he also must have trusted me a little to show it to me – or, at least, he must not have seen me as any kind of threat. I wanted to build on his trust, and I didn't have much to go on, so I didn't hurry things.

He had some strange habits. As we walked around, sometimes he would raise his leg and urinate against a tree like a dog. Once he squatted and defecated in front of me, continuing to talk as if nothing had happened. He showed me caches which he had laid down in previous years containing bottles of water, dry foods and wraps of heroin; it seemed he anticipated trouble from creditors on the coast, which might mean he had to leave his cabin at short notice. Whether these men were real, or just shadows of his mind, it was impossible to know, but if I was going to have any chance of finding out more about Bowen and finding his stash, Antar was still my only lead. Antar seemed able to talk about almost anything, but he rarely showed much real interest in what he was saying. When he spoke there was usually a faraway look in his eyes. The only topic which seemed to draw him out of his stupor was America: whenever it was mentioned, his face immediately clouded over and a bitter look came over him, as if someone had brought a vile smell into the room. Once he even spat on the ground in disgust. Probably, knowing about my long imprisonment, he felt he could vent this hatred openly with me and that it was something we shared; but his strength of feeling struck me as odd, since he otherwise appeared to have no interest in anything political.

As the weeks passed, it became increasingly clear to me that Antar's friendship with Bowen had never been a particularly close one. They had in fact only known each other a little in Madrid in the old days, when Bowen had worked there for one of the fine-art auction houses. The friendship had been kept up only intermittently, and probably only because they'd both been better men in those days, and wanted to be faithful to an earlier memory of themselves. I began to wonder whether Antar had overstated the extent of his connection to Bowen in order to wheedle payouts from Purse's people – or whether this friendship might even be something existing largely in Antar's mind. Could I trust what Antar was telling me? I wasn't sure but, as he was my only source, I really didn't have much choice.

In the end, though, Antar did show me something relevant and memorable. When he told me to meet him the night before I left for Madrid, in an empty lot behind the

New Golden Mile, I almost decided not to go; his morose company was starting to take its toll on my own morale. But I turned up. As we stood in the lot, all around us were the barren, scrubby hills, and on their crests were the skeletons of buildings left behind by the tide of the last construction boom. Most of the tracks between the buildings were overgrown, and blocked by piles of building materials; but Antar knew where he was going.

Ahead was the shell of a building, just like the others, a desolate heap of a thing: the scene of Bowen's death. Looking at it, I understood why everyone had been so certain that it was an accident. The structure was entirely open to the sky, and anyone standing within it would have been as obvious as a sculpture on a plinth. It would have been impossible for someone else to be up there with Bowen when he fell, and not be seen.

An air of damnation seemed still to cling to the place: cracked concrete was pierced through with creepers, and rusted plant lay to one side where cattle birds had nested. We must have sat there for an hour, and at some point Antar turned away from me and began to sob. Somehow I knew he was not really weeping for Bowen, for me, or even for himself. It was simply an expression of how he always felt inside.

10

My enthusiasm for this apparent wild goose chase had not waned, as I was again coming under serious financial pressure. I seemed unable to curb the habit of spending money as soon as I had it. If anything, I was more desperate than ever to put my finances in order, but my leads were already running dry, and I was starting to wonder whether I should go back to my day job of writing.

The auction house in Madrid where Antar had told me that Bowen had once worked was not difficult to find; it was right in the centre of town, on the corner of the Plaza de la Independencia and opposite the Retiropark. But the day I called, the staff were all at a sale for bullfighting memorabilia two blocks away, on the ground floor of the Ritz Hotel. The walls were hung with bulls' heads, matadors' costumes, capes and *bandaleros*, with faded prints at the back showing the origins of the sport in cavalry exercises and slaughterhouse rituals. The room was packed out with local dealers, and most of the small auction-house staff were occupied taking telephone bids on a desk to one side.

I had a word with each of them after the sale was over, when they all remained behind in the room to pack the pieces into special rubber-lined boxes. Only a couple of them, it turned out – one of the Old Masters' experts and his assistant – had been there in Bowen's day, and neither had worked in the same department nor admitted to remembering much about him. They only knew of one friend of Bowen's still left in the city: an antiquarian book dealer called Ralph Drake.

I had met Drake a few times socially on visits to the city back in the eighties, and I still had numbers for friends of his. Only a few hours after leaving the sale, I managed to contact him from my hotel on Plaza Neptuno. If ever I needed a reminder that smuggling was a tight community then this was it.

Being aware that in the old days Drake had been in the same line as myself immediately made me wonder if his relationship with Bowen might also have been a professional one; but I wasn't hopeful that he would tell me much. I remembered him as quite slippery and evasive. He was one of those slim public-school types that one would always see at expat gatherings, who always wore a hand-made suit but still looked the worse for wear, and gave the impression of being there for the drink and not much else. He sounded rather surprised to hear from me out of the blue, but agreed to meet me the following evening at a tapas bar in the old town.

It was one of the semi-subterranean cellars behind the Plaza Mayor, which always seemed almost empty despite being so central. Presumably Drake had chosen it for this reason. He was already there, waiting in a booth at the back, and it was difficult to ignore how unwell he looked. Last time I had seen him, a decade previously, he had still had something of a reputation as a ladies' man – he had briefly squired a number of high-profile actresses as well as some of the girls whose pictures one used to see in the society pages at the back of *Tatler* and *Harper's*. Now he was painfully thin, and his skin had the unmistakable yellowish hue of advanced liver disease.

When I explained that I wanted to trace Bowen's last movements, Drake reacted with unease. For a while he avoided the subject, and we spoke in an uncommitted sort of way about mutual friends; when I tried to steer the conversation back to Bowen, he avoided eye contact and clammed up. I suspected he had already been paid for information about Bowen by Purse, in the course of his enquiries after Bowen's death. The other possibility was that he was involved with others who were looking for Bowen's stash – perhaps even on the basis that he spoke to no one else about him. So when I made him a financial proposition of my own and he said he had to go to another appointment, suggesting that we meet the following day, I took this as indication that it was something he would have to sleep on. Either that, or he had to get clearance from others higher up.

When we met the next day, Drake came straight to the point. He rejected the offer I had made him for information, making it clear that he would only be willing to talk about Bowen on another quid pro quo basis. What he really wanted was for me to come in with him on an ecstasy scam.

At this point my heart sank. While Drake was erudite and charming, he had a most unreliable reputation in business. It was well known that over the years he had dabbled in ecstasy to prop up his book-buying funds – he was keen on early printed books and rare incunabula, books printed prior to the advent of mechanized presses, many of which he had smuggled out of Spain in fruit trucks for his own collection rather than selling on. Most of his previous scams had ended badly.

Nevertheless, I listened as he explained he was expecting a delivery of MDMA powder shortly to a locker at Zurich airport. It was enough to press a million pills and was coming from a lab in Hyderabad, India, where the equipment of a legitimate pharma company was being used overnight to turn out the pills. It sounded like a lot, but in reality this was a medium-sized deal, compact enough for him to make a case for muling the powder by air. Where I came in was that he wanted me to press it using equipment I would have to source, then sell it on to some contacts of his on the rave scene in England. Prices there were still about 30 per cent more than on the continent. He wanted this done within a month, and he was expecting a minimum return for himself agreed in advance.

There were several aspects of this I did not like at all. Since the introduction of specialist sniffer dogs, muling anything by air was a fool's game, virtually suicidal. Added to which, presses were heavy, usually weighing over a ton, and their movements were often tracked by the police with transponders, which could easily be concealed on something so bulky. As I did not know Drake's buyers or whether they had heat on them, the whole thing felt toxic. I even wondered briefly whether Drake might deliberately be attempting to endanger me, drawing me into a risky scheme on behalf of someone else who was interested in Bowen's stash and wanted me out of the picture.

But the more he talked, the clearer it seemed that this was a badly conceived plan rather than anything more sinister. I told Drake that I was willing to do it, but only in my own way, and that I wanted to wait until the start of the skiing season the following autumn, as there was a firm I knew that brought in cocaine in adapted ski gear, and their experts could be used. The head of this firm, Paul Jacobs, was an associate of my former partner, Old John, so I knew he was a relatively safe pair of hands. I also explained that I wanted the pills encapsulated, not pressed, as the equipment to do this was small and easily obtained; and that the buyers would be my own contacts. I stipulated that the job had to be done in two runs rather than one, due to the quantity involved and the difficulties in recruiting reliable couriers. I was hoping that all these conditions would be enough to put Drake off the idea altogether.

Predictably, Drake then made a lot out of the significant price difference between pills and capsules, and held out for a press; but after an hour's further discussion, during which it was clear I was not going to compromise on anything else, he reluctantly agreed to the rest. He was old-school enough to want to shake on it. I hesitated for a moment when he held out his hand, but then it was done. 'Now,' I said, 'tell me about Bowen.'

We finished our drinks, and Drake led me through the medieval streets to a narrow lane behind the Plaza Santa Ana. There, he showed me Bowen's old apartment from the outside.

It was on the corner of Calle del Prado and Leon, and on either side were pay-by-the-hour hotels and dingy-looking bars. 'It was a lot worse back in those days,' Drake commented as we stood on the pavement opposite the building, taking in the scene.

Drake told me the building had been used as a storehouse by the auction company. He knew all this because Bowen had lived there for virtually no rent, in the early eighties; there were still several rusted alarms and heavy shutters over the door from the days when it had been a store. Drake took me round to the back, where he said Bowen had occupied a couple of rooms, but there wasn't much more to see from that angle.

Drake seemed sure that Bowen had never received any visitors while he lived there, and that out of office hours Bowen had been a virtual recluse. Finally I was getting new information that would help me put together a picture of Bowen. According to Drake, Bowen had been one of that first idealistic generation of ecstasy smugglers who'd had the field to themselves in the late seventies and early eighties, along with Juan Royal in Houston and Spencer Purse in Ibiza; all originating from the same circle as Alexander Shulgin, who had rediscovered ecstasy in Berkeley in the seventies. They had all started out true believers who genuinely thought ecstasy would change the world, but in the years after the Barcelona conference, the rules of the game had changed. The drug had moved out from the ghetto of the hippies in the Bay Area and Texas and the gay clubs to become a global clubbing phenomenon, the most valuable ingestible substance by weight on the planet. It had become a global business, with all the pressures for profit that entailed. Bowen had ridden this tiger, and become a rich man in the process. However, being a founding father had never quite lost its aura, and he had always carried that with him; whatever it is, there is something special about being the first to market. I thought I knew what Bowen must have felt. It made you a prophet of sorts, and standing there, looking up at the apartment he had once occupied, I could feel the power of it still.

From the apartment, Drake walked me down to a bar on Leon, that long, narrow, sunless street, and showed me a catalogue from the auction house that he had rolled up in his coat. At the back was a map of the world, and in every major capital the company had an office or representative. He explained that works of art could be valued in one country, shipped to another for an appraisal, then consigned for sale in a third. To do all this, the auction house had evolved its own international shipping network, and to be on the inside of something like that, pulling the levers, was not a bad place to be if you were a smuggler. What was now becoming clearer was that Bowen's scam, like all good scams, had been at its heart a simple one. When artworks came into Customs they were checked for their documentation, specifically whether they had the correct export licences and were not infringing patrimonial laws. The high values of the items blinded the inspectors to the possibility that there could be anything present but the items themselves; but once the paperwork was checked and the work moved to the store, there was nothing preventing the shadowy entity which had consigned the work from simply withdrawing it from sale, and unloading anything it contained. I couldn't help but smile at the beauty of it. This was just the kind of scam that I would have been proud to pull off myself.

Drake believed that Bowen had taken his job at the shipping department of the auction house because he had already planned to parasite its network. It was a scam almost in plain sight, well-adapted to the early days when ecstasy was a low-volume, high-margin business catering to metropolitan elites. But as profits spiralled, so the volumes produced outgrew the system that had created them. Only so many pills could fit into an armoire or piece of sculpture, and when new, more popular markets were needed, Bowen had moved on and out of Spain.

It was at this point, Drake admitted, that his knowledge of Bowen and his scam ended. They had no longer had much contact after Bowen left Madrid, and the rest of what he could tell me was only sketchy. As far as he knew, Bowen had continued to work in trusted positions within the art world, first at the Tate Gallery in London, then for a leading specialist art courier company, one of the museum's contractors, and had operated alone in his later scams without any partners or an organization around him. I took a mental note of all this, knowing it might be useful later.

I told Drake I would be in touch once I was back in London. As we said our farewells at the bottom of the Calle del Prado, with all the civil servants rushing past us

from the parliament building, I thought I could sense a
certain relief in him as he left me – as if he had finished
playing a role he was not comfortable with. While we
stayed in touch by phone, it was the last time that I would
see him.

I spent my last days in Madrid hanging around
Bowen's old neighbourhood, and sat in the same cheap
bars and cinemas he must have passed every day. But if I
was hoping to stumble across some further insights – some
moment of possession, maybe, a haunting of sorts – I was
to be disappointed. It seemed that I really had reached a
dead end this time. I could not honestly say I had any
clearer sense of the man, and I had now got myself
caught up in a scam that I wanted absolutely nothing to
do with.

On the final day, I persuaded the doorman to let me
into Bowen's old apartment. His lack of surprise suggested
I was not the first to make such a request, and that others
had probably been there when the trail had still been
warm. The front of the apartment block was being used as
a storeroom for bouquets of plastic flowers. I had time
enough alone to search it thoroughly, but there was nothing left from the days when the auction house had used it
except a few broken frames and old catalogues. The rooms
at the end, where Bowen must have eaten and slept alone,
were small and equally empty. It didn't take long to satisfy
myself that there had probably never been anything there.

I came away feeling that I had wasted my energy. Was it time, at last, for me to make a tentative return to public life?

11

It was the late spring of 1998 when I finally decided it was safe to come out of hiding and go back to London. I had wasted almost eight months kicking my heels in Spain chasing after Bowen's shadow, and I had nothing to show for it. When I'd left London my bank account had been in rude health for the first time in years, thanks to the sales of the book; but after chasing my tail for so long, even those funds were now running low.

The blowback from my association in the press with the Montreal scam had now died down, and I felt it was safe to operate publicly again. During this time it had not been safe for me to return home except for fleeting visits, and I made a trip to La Vileta before returning to London in April 1998. Although the official promotional commitments for my autobiography were over, I had devised a stage show based on the book, which I had tried out on audiences the previous year and which I hoped would generate a modest additional revenue stream. It opened with a documentary about my years on the run in the eighties, and continued with improvisations and sketches. Over the next few months the show toured the main UK cities; mostly it was sold out. At the very least, it never failed to cover its costs, and some books were usually sold afterwards when I did signings.

These shows consolidated my public image as an amiable pothead – an image I did nothing to discourage – and I continued to make regular appearances on behalf of the Legalise Cannabis Alliance. Guesting as a DJ across the country, I conspicuously smoked pot in public venues, and on one occasion I entered Marylebone police station with joints, challenging them to arrest me. At this time, the Blair government were advertising for the position of Drugs Tsar, a nationwide coordinator of drugs policy; my application of course got turned down, but all this provided more material for the shows, and although this had not been my original intention, I found these activities were now providing me with a rather useful cover for my more clandestine trade. In the past, such stunts would have been a magnet for police surveillance and a shortcut to an MI5 file, but times had changed: 1998 was the second year of Tony Blair's New Labour government, and so-called *Cool Britannia* was in full swing. Rank-and-file cops no longer had an appetite for busting casual tokers and ruining their lives with a police record, while senior officers preferred to allocate funds to weightier matters. In fact, I became convinced there was really no better look at this time for a smuggler than being a public pothead.

As I toured the country, this was largely the image I projected. It was not a difficult act to pull off, partly because of who I was, but also because it was clear that most of my audience were coming along stoned with the expectation of seeing precisely such a figure. Of course, I could not disappoint them. Though it was difficult to see the audience clearly through the blinding spotlights, I was able to get a look at them during intervals and book signings. The majority were in their late teens and twenties and looked as innocent as lambs – exactly the kinds of people who were now filling the clubs and bars in Ibiza. Little did they know that their lives and mine were about to become doubly entwined. Their heckling was tame and good-natured, and often afterwards some of them would come to my room for a smoke. Mostly these were earnest young growers challenging me to sample their produce; they brought skunk they had grown hydroponically in attics or outhouses, and seemed to regard my presence as some sort of provocation to get me as stoned as they could. The THC levels in this gear were far higher than in the Lebanese and Pakistani I was accustomed to, and as a result I was often left the worse for wear. But it was all harmless fun, and I enjoyed the company and retelling my stories from my old smuggling days before prison.

That summer, I was asked to judge a national marijuana growers' competition in Salford. It was being held in a pub after closing time. The judging involved sitting in a sealed basement with a row of pre-loaded bongs, sampling each and marking them for flavour and effect. Afterwards I was meant to give an interview, but being starved of oxygen for over two hours had taken its toll, and halfway through I found myself on the verge of passing out. The next week, three more invitations came to judge further national growers' competitions, all of which I accepted with pleasure. On one of these occasions I was driven to a venue called the Stonemasons, near Stoner Park (I presumed that these places had been chosen for their names). Again, there was a sealed basement and a row of bongs; but I was now more circumspect in my consumption, like a wine taster, and managed to leave on my own two feet and walking in a straight line.

By the third week, invitations to judge growing competitions were coming in so thick and fast that I had to start turning them down. Theoretically there should have been only one national dope-growing competition, in the same way there is a single national competition for show-dogs or single national figure-skating championships. However, as each growing event was necessarily clandestine, there was no bar to any two-bit competition claiming to be a national event. In the Greater Manchester area alone I counted five such competitions in a six-week period. I began to come across inferior product grown by Vietnamese gangs, claiming to be a 'national winner', with a fake endorsement from me on the packet. I was amused to see that my notoriety had developed to this level, and couldn't help but wonder what Agent Lovano of the DEA, who had spent six years of his life in pursuit of me, would have made of all of this.

Although I stopped accepting judging invitations, eager growers continued to come to my dressing room after shows bearing offerings of bongs loaded with near-lethal doses of skunk. My endorsement would significantly raise the price they could charge for their dope, so they were highly motivated. Invariably these young men and women, who were making significant amounts of money out of the enterprise, were even more stoned than I was, and would not take no for an answer.

It was notable that the police never turned up at any of my public appearances, despite the fact that dope was invariably being consumed by me and members of the audience. In fact, the only time any police came to my dressing room they were in plain clothes and hoping to get a book signed, or a photograph with me. I learned from an ex-drug-squad friend that this lack of intervention was a deliberate policy – presumably simply to deny me publicity, rather than lull me into any false sense of security about surveillance. But of course I could not be sure, and the warning of the Scotland Yard officers at Gatwick that they would be watching me was always in the back of my mind. In my experience, the police did not make empty threats.

Also preying on my mind was my involvement with Drake. Hardly a day went by when I didn't regret getting drawn into his scheme. I felt bound to honour our agreement and knew it would be fatal for my reputation if I did not – but this didn't stop me hoping there might be some way out of it that would be acceptable to him. By now any expectations that Drake might provide further useful leads about Bowen's stash had faded, and given his poor health, my hopes were pinned on his becoming too unwell to continue with the scam. The touring was providing a reasonable excuse for putting off the date, so as the months passed I kept adding more shows and engagements of various sorts, keeping him informed of this in the hope he might lose patience and decide to use someone else.

Just to be on the safe side, however, I contacted Paul Jacobs, who ran the ski-gear firm and who was the only person I knew still running drug couriers from Switzerland. I brought him up to speed and told him what was potentially involved, so that at least he would be prepared if the scam ever happened. He listened patiently, and we agreed basic terms if it ever did come together.

At the same time, I also left a message for Nick Salomon, right-hand man of Spencer Purse, who ran Ibiza.

Purse was still the largest and most established buyer on the island, and it seemed inevitable that I'd have to deal with him at some point in order to shift the pills, so it seemed wise to get ahead of myself and talk to him. I mentioned the quantity and a rough delivery date, but I hoped that I would not have to follow through with either at this stage, so did not make any firm commitments to either party that would lead to disappointment later. Salomon was enthusiastic, but businesslike, as he knew as well as I did that until the first stages of the scam had been put in place, all the talk was hypothetical.

It was now nearing the end of the summer of 1998. My tour, which had started at the Shepherd's Bush Empire (where my run had been longer than Abba's), ended in Edinburgh, with back-to-back shows at the Pleasance to meet demand. I had judged half a dozen so-called national dope-growing competitions, and throughout all of this I had been developing my argument for the legalization of cannabis.

The most popular argument in favour of legalization had always been that marijuana, like most recreational drugs, was no more harmful to physical or mental health than tobacco or alcohol. Therefore, the argument went, marijuana and drugs like it should be licensed in the same way as those substances. The product would then become more standardized and safer, and the government would gain large additional tax revenues which could be put towards building schools and hospitals.

I did not like this argument, as it conceded that recreational drugs were in themselves as harmful as tobacco and alcohol, which implied that in a perfect world people would not be taking them. Strong lobbies were already pushing for tobacco or alcohol use to be curtailed. If this happened, as seemed inevitable, then of course any argument for marijuana legalization due to parity of harm with tobacco and alcohol would not stand.

The libertarian argument potentially had the same flaw: it offered that the state had no right to curtail an individual's freedom of choice by legislation, so long as individual actions did not compromise the freedom of others. It did not argue that marijuana was a force for good, or even that it was not harmful; instead it placed recreational drugs in a category of unsafe actions that an individual had the right to engage in from a position of informed consent. In this same category were dangerous sports like boxing, or self-harming acts like suicide.

The problem was that one could always find ways in which these activities did, in fact, compromise the freedom of others. Boxing, it could be argued, generated long-term medical problems, which in turn fell on the national health budget and deprived others of care. The same argument could be made against dope, or almost anything, when one put one's mind to it. It was only a small step from saying people should do what they wanted if it did not compromise the freedoms of others, to saying that what they wanted was selfish and destructive. Taken to its logical limits, libertarianism became the back-door route to a police state.

My line was always simply that cannabis would be safer to society if legalized and controlled rather than distributed by the criminal fraternity. I was willing to accept that cannabis was not completely harmless, that it was mildly addictive, and was an unsuitable recreational drug for some people. The most persuasive arguments for legalization were always negative ones; one simply had to look at arguments for banning dope, and hold them up to the light, and at this point they usually looked ridiculous.

What most people don't know is that marijuana had only been banned in the first place by a stroke of bad luck. When the League of Nations had met in 1925 to decide which drugs should be outlawed, enemy number one had been opium. Marijuana had not even been on the agenda. Unfortunately the Egyptian delegate – a certain Mohammad El-Guindy, apparently a heavy opium user who was trying to save himself – had held the floor for almost an hour, giving a wild account of the dangers of marijuana, and by the time he was finished everyone was convinced marijuana was more dangerous than opium. The argument he put forward was that hashish led to sloth, concupiscence and ravenousness, and ultimately to madness. However, when I looked at the changes in Egypt's mental health statistics after it was banned, it appeared they had only become worse.

In my heart, though, I was not really interested in arguments around whether certain drugs should be banned or not. What mattered to me was that people enjoyed them and wanted to buy them. I had always been in favour of legalizing cannabis, even when my livelihood depended on its illegality – rather like a doctor, who is dependent on disease for his income but would still welcome the discovery of a universal panacea. Every night, I took to the stage and repeated a version of these arguments. Inevitably I got into a version of the same heated discussion, but I liked to think that my message was getting across. Most events ended in a standing ovation – not for me, but for the very public position I was taking.

As I toured, I was staying almost every night in a different hotel; except they might as well have been the same hotel, because all the rooms were alike. To save money, I stayed at motels like Premier Inn, Travelodge or Jurys Inn. At this time they still had smoking rooms, but these had to be booked in advance, so often I found myself in non-smoking rooms and had to disable the smoke alarm by sealing it in a plastic bag or a condom. Having done this, I would collapse on the bed in my clothes, too exhausted to do much more. Sometimes I would fall asleep without even undressing; mostly I just lay and watched television in a daze for about an hour, too tired even to call home for more than a few minutes.

But however tired I was, the last thing I always did was to look at an empty postcard from the Marbella Club Hotel that I had picked up in one of the bars in Spain. It showed the three-grand-a-night chalets where Bowen had stayed, and around them in the background the lush semi-tropical gardens. The story I had been told was that the hotel had been built after a German socialite, Prince Alfonso Hohenloe, had broken down in his Rolls-Royce in the woods west of Marbella just after the war. He had been so taken with the beauty of the spot, nestled amid the pines and rocky coves, that he had stayed put. He decided to have a villa built there where all his friends could come to stay, and so many had been entranced by the beauty of the place that it had gradually grown into a hotel.

I did not really expect to learn anything from the card, but whatever the truth about Bowen's stash, this postcard became the source of endless daydreaming – a habit that I had refined over many hours of boredom lying on my bed in prison. I didn't even know which chalet had been Bowen's. Close up, the gardens were just abstract colours, nothing one could recognize as solid forms or shapes – a bit like Bowen himself, in that regard. The closer one looked, the vaguer the shape of him seemed to become, and the more he seemed just to disappear from view.

12

By the start of September 1998 there was still no sign of
Drake's health deteriorating to the point of cancelling our
scheme, and I had no choice but to begin preparing. The
significant risks involved in air muling weighed heavily on
my mind. It was that section of the scam that I focused on
first with Paul Jacobs from the ski-gear firm: every day I
was in London, which was the hub of my touring, Jacobs
came to my room at the Groucho Club with large bags
from Lillywhites. Various pieces of ski equipment, boots,
boards and jackets were disassembled, filled with pure
vitamin C ascorbic acid powder and put back together
again. In the evenings we went down to the City, where a
friend of Jacobs manned a security entrance to one of the
banks, and the items were fed through the X-ray and the
images studied. If prison had taught me one thing, it was
that you could never be too well prepared.

Jacobs was of the view that the equipment was so
diverse in design that customs officers would not spot
anomalies between the interiors of the same items, and

he pointed out that the powder was not radiopaque, so would show only as a void within the plastics, not as something solid. I was not so confident about this. To reassure me, he recommended three couriers he had previously worked with, who were willing to carry the gear for suitable remuneration. He would not give me their names, probably because he thought I might hire them directly and cut him out, but he vouched for them as being reliable in runs he had done on similar routes.

Jacobs assured me they all passed well as skiers back from a weekend – in fact, this was basically what they were, the courier work being just a sideline for them. As a further precaution, he wanted to use a sniffer dog to check that there was no smell that could be picked up by the dogs at either airport. Although hiring such dogs was costly as well as troublesome, and I had always thought that electronic sensors could do the job more reliably, to keep Jacobs sweet, a dog was arranged through a former associate of Dennis Watkins in Milton Keynes.

Jacobs also wanted to use a cottage that a friend of his rented in Suffolk to receive the couriers, and for the pressing. I held out for using several cottages, for reasons I would explain to him later. We ordered brochures from holiday-let companies, using false names. Just as I had always done, in the usual way, a shortlist was drawn up of places that were both remote and not overlooked. At my insistence Jacobs agreed not to take any other jobs over the next two months, so that there would be no heat from his side.

I had no real way of checking that Jacobs was not doing other things on the side, but it was in his interest not to endanger the scam, and my reckoning was that the bigger the slice Jacobs got, the more unlikely he was to get distracted. I was aware that he did not in fact have the best of reputations in smuggling circles because of his un-social, spiky character, but I believed this was unwarranted and was willing to give him the benefit of the doubt. Jacobs was a bit of a cold fish, and people found him dif-ficult – but most of the time he just kept his head down and acted professionally, which was the only thing that really mattered.

On the surface we had little in common. He did not drink or smoke and never took drugs of any sort, except for professional reasons such as when sampling goods. The large, nerdy glasses which made him look like an accountant or IT technician weren't a cover, and his only real passion seemed to be collecting old industrial machin-ery, which he took apart and then put back together again (Frankensteining, as he called it) in his garden in the sub-urbs. He also knew a lot about genetics, and always had a book with him on the subject. In idle moments he would sometimes pick it up and read rather than chatting, which some found off-putting. But he had learned his craft in his youth as an assistant to my former partner, Old John, and this connection meant that his trustworthiness was beyond reproach as far as I was concerned.

Another thing in Jacobs' favour was that he was one of the few former hashish smugglers who had successfully diversified into cocaine, the distribution of which was normally controlled by the West Indian gangs. This meant that he had experience in bringing into the country high-grade cocaine processed in a Swiss lab, rather than the usual bush labs, for distribution in London media circles. He was also one of the few smugglers left who still had experience running couriers. To have survived in such a high-risk game meant that he was something of a perfectionist, a stickler for quality, and he insisted his product was only cut with pharmaceutical-grade ascorbic acid rather than baby powder or amphetamines. He also insisted on selling only to established dealers who worked in the West End, even going so far as to check on them occasionally to see the gear had not been cut further. By the late 1990s most of the gear coming into the Groucho, Soho House, Blacks, the newly reopened Criterion and the other West End media clubs was coming in via Jacobs; so if you were one of the many people cutting lines there in that period, the odds are that it came from him. However, to look at him you would never have guessed it in a thousand years, and when he turned up to see me in my room at the Groucho, he told me that the front desk thought he was one of the guys who maintained the computers.

In the autumn of 1998, as we were preparing the scam, Jacobs and I spent a great deal of time together. But it was difficult to get much out of him. If he didn't just disappear into one of his books, his preferred topic was genetic ancestry, and he was not shy, whenever we were not talking shop, of subjecting me to long and technical lectures on his cod-philosophy. His theory was that all humanity was descended from a single mother, 'Eve', who had crossed out of Africa into modern-day Yemen on the Arabian peninsula. While some of her children had turned right and grown into the Asian peoples, the others had turned left and become the Europeans. All of the latter were descended from a single gene pool in northern Turkey, which had contained the genes for fair hair and for the tolerance of lactose, which in turn had allowed them to survive the harsh winters by supplementing their diets with animal milk. When these early Turks had crossed the Bosporus, they had again divided in two directions: one group had gone along the shore to become the Mediterranean peoples, and the other had floated up the Danube on rafts to become the Northern Europeans.

But Jacobs insisted there was one anomaly to this pattern: he thought the Celtic peoples were in fact descended from migrants who had crossed over into Europe, not by the traditional Turkish route, but over the Straits of Gibraltar. Skeletal remains in the caves of the Rock, he claimed, showed that this was already a route used by

Neanderthals, and though there had been interbreeding with the other European races, which disguised this, careful parsing of the genetic record showed that the Celts were closely related to the modern-day Berber people of North Africa. Ancient potsherds described a direct lineage back to an ancient civilization lost under the waters where the islands of Palma and Tenerife stood today. The Celts had, according to Jacobs, been refugees from the earthquake that had destroyed the paradisiacal cities of Atlantis, and the Celtic myths and culture were our last link back to that lost world; so that all the melancholy and distant longing among the Celts was the sadness of an original exile from paradise.

This all sounded a bit far-fetched, like the stuff the hangers-on around Old John would spout after smoking Nepalese. My suspicion was that this was where Jacobs had picked it up. Although I'd listened to a fair amount of stoned bollocks in my time and was willing to put up with it, Jacobs did not even have the excuse of being stoned when he came out with it all. What it did do, though, was remind me how much I missed my friend Old John, whose ramblings along the same lines had been the source of much entertainment during the long hours of waiting around for deals to come through.

Jacobs would offer that the Welsh were descended from a race of alien poets who had founded Atlantis, and when I chided him for this sort of daft talk, he would say he'd had it from Old John himself – who he claimed had never smoked anything other than Tom Thumb cigars and Indian *bidis*, nor taken any other intoxicants apart from brandy or wine. Bizarrely, this was true, but it did not lend any greater credibility to these wacky theories, made worse by Jacobs constantly repeating himself. Out of respect for Old John's memory, as well as to keep Jacobs on side as much as possible as we drew closer to the crucial part of the scam, I never pressed him too hard, although it was a job not to roll my eyes.

My feeling was that Jacobs was better kept out of any negotiating with buyers, so when we had finished planning the packing and transport I contacted the buyer myself to discuss the back end of the scam. I had selected Spencer Purse because he was one of the oldest and most respected names in the trade. Although I'd never worked with him myself, I had known him since the eighties, when he had worked with associates of mine, so it felt like a step back in time. During our brief initial conversation I'd informed Purse's right-hand man, Nick Salomon, about the volume involved and that I wanted a belly-to-belly cash deal. But Salomon came back with a ridiculously low figure, and even after wriggling him up a few basic points, it was difficult to see how we were going to cover even the minimum return Drake had secured.

The reality was that Salomon and Purse simply did not need my business. They had made astronomical profits from riding the rave scene of the eighties and early nineties. The stories I had heard involved them leaving with bags of cash so large, they would often have to bury some and come back the next day. They were still moving hundreds of thousands of pills each weekend in raves across the world. Their apparent lack of interest was confirmed at my second meeting with Salomon, when he gave me the standard line about Vietnamese over-production and adulterated product pulling down margins. He seemed on the verge of walking away when I pressed for a higher number.

We were in Battersea Park, across the river from Salomon's house in Chelsea. The last time I had seen Salomon, he had looked like a rave DJ, decked out in all the latest urban gear. Now he was wearing a coat with a velvet collar, and looked like a City executive. By contrast, I felt like a hippie throwback with my long hair and summer shirt. For the next half hour, repeatedly glancing at his watch as if he had more important things to attend to, he filled me in on the rest of his property portfolio. The list was so long he had trouble remembering it all. It included an organic farm in the Cotswolds, a penthouse on Copacabana, and one of the finest villas on the north coast of Ibiza. Only at the end did he get back to business, again naming a humiliatingly low price, while all the time looking at me as if he did not care in the least whether the deal stuck.

'We're talking about pure powder pills, remember,'

I reminded him, affecting easy confidence. 'They're as rare as unicorns.'

Salomon did not look at all impressed; but then something strange happened. He got on the phone, presumably to Purse, though maybe to no one at all, and came back to me with a fairy-tale figure. I was not quite sure what had changed between us, but the new figure – hundreds of thousands of pounds – was much higher than I had hoped for. It was difficult to imagine they could have broken even at that level, but that was not my problem. 'One condition,' said Salomon, casually, just as the thrill of this apparent victory was spreading through me. 'You deliver everything to Purse yourself, OK? In person.'

I didn't like the sound of this at all. With my face on half the tube stations in London as part of advertising for *Mr Nice*, I would be recognized immediately if anything went wrong. I pointed this out to Salomon. 'Let's say I'll meet Purse first and then deliver later. I'll sort out a safe place and time.'

Salomon looked at me for a moment, then nodded. 'OK.' His tone was courteous now, relaxed. He gave me a number to call, saying almost casually, 'Just give us a few hours' notice,' which also struck me as odd. Usually, people in our business wanted as much notice as possible to prepare carefully for all eventualities. A few hours' notice on big consignments was virtually unheard of. But without skipping a beat, he reassured me that this was how they always did it to keep the information loop as tight as possible and to make their movements more difficult to track. Given the figure they had now offered and their level of experience, it was something I knew I would just have to swallow. After all our months of preparation, and hours spent working out every eventuality, the scam was now set.

13

Now that the pieces of the puzzle were in place and we just had to finalize the timings, I turned my attention back to finding Bowen's stash, more convinced than ever that it could be a ticket to long-term financial security. That said, I could not shake a deep sense of foreboding. I felt I was now swimming in currents whose source might always elude me, but I knew I was too far in, and if I attempted to swim away it could be more dangerous still. Looking back, maybe I could still have walked and lain low for a while, but sometimes the only way to the light seems to lie through a place of greater darkness. It was in this spirit that I began to find out all I could about Bowen's earlier years in the hope that would turn up something that would help me though the impasse I now found myself in.

I started with Alexander Shulgin, the pioneering chemist and researcher into psychedelics, and the circle around him. Given that Bowen had originally emerged from this small group, I expected to come across references to him in this material. But after considerable research, all I could turn up was one line, and any direct connection to Bowen was vague to say the least. It was in a chemistry journal in the back stacks at the London Library. Most of the article was just abstruse equations relating to Shulgin's original synthesis of ecstasy, and an account of how a Schedule I licence from the DEA had authorized this work in return for his consulting with the agency. Only at the end, where there were informal notes on some of Shulgin's assistants and hangers-on (including Leo Zeff, the psychologist who would first give the drug to his patients in San Francisco), was there a fleeting mention of Bowen, described as 'the experimental chemist Henry Bow [sic], who later cut all ties to the group'. The chances of Bowen having changed his name, as I had done numerous times myself, were high. It was also very possible that there had been a clerical error. What gave me some hope was that the chronology of events stacked up perfectly.

I knew the chances were that this was probably a reference to Bowen, but strangely, the more I thought about this line – and I thought about it a lot – the more certain I became that I had not understood it correctly.

At first, I inferred that Bowen had not really cut ties with the group, but that they had cut ties with him – that they had felt Bowen had betrayed them by going into the commercial ecstasy business, like Juan Royal and Spencer Purse. But as time went by, I was no longer so sure about this. It was also plausible that Bowen had cut ties with the group for his own safety because he had gone underground and become a smuggler. The more research I carried out, the more I suspected it meant something more worrying. Given that I was now as caught up in it as I was, the events which followed my return to London from doing some further shows in the north would only make this clearer to me.

On my first night back, I had waited for the rush-hour traffic to pass, then taken a taxi to the Embankment to a place from which there was a view of the tall, slightly ungainly facade of the Tate Gallery. I had hitherto known the building only in the innocent context of a useful place for lunch or for meeting friends. Now it would take on a more urgent, almost sinister character; I could not bring myself to get any closer, but just stood and stared at it. Drake had told me that Bowen had worked at the museum until a few months before his death. Bearing in mind my interpretations of the line about Bowen in the chemistry journal, I now felt privately certain that his activities there were in some way integral to his final scam.

The Tate Gallery (now Tate Britain), one of the most established art museums in London, was not the sort of place one could just wander into and begin asking delicate questions. My attempts to talk to the staff led nowhere, and even former employees who I tracked down were tight-lipped and said they could hardly remember Bowen.

All I learned was that he had been a full-time staffer for less than a year, until the department he had worked for had been reorganized in the ongoing move to Tate Modern on the South Bank. After that, he had worked for a specialist art shipping company, one of the museum's regular contractors. Bearing in mind the high value and fragility of what they handled, the staff there would be extremely carefully vetted, and I knew the chances of getting any information from them were low.

Sure enough, when I went to the shipping company's offices posing as a prospective client and tried to talk to people, I was told that contact between staff and outsiders was discouraged for security reasons. The manager was an ex-military type, and I got the impression not much slipped by him; he seemed wary of me and uneasy in my company, as if he sensed that I was not who I claimed to be. It struck me as unlikely that Bowen would have stored anything under the watchful eye of such a person; and from what I could see of the temporary storage pens and the garage area, they were kept clutter-free. With all the cameras around and so many comings and goings, there were no suitable hiding places here for a smuggler looking to hide considerable volumes of drugs.

The only lead I came away with was the information that someone had recently been fired from the place. All the staff had to sign legal forms agreeing not to smoke or drink while at work, and apparently the person in question had been seen smoking a few metres from his van. He had been fired without so much as a warning. I didn't hold out much hope that this would lead anywhere, but I asked Jacobs to ring up the company pretending to be the man's father and try to wangle a forwarding address. The plan was that Jacobs would attempt to play on any embittered feelings over the sacking, and if this failed, offer money for information. We agreed a sum in advance and arranged to speak later in the week.

It was at this point that events took a sinister turn. When I got back in from speaking to Jacobs on a payphone, my room at the club looked somehow wrong. Nothing was taken or broken, but in the couple of hours I had been out at the storage company, things had definitely been moved. Someone was on to me. I was familiar with the patterns room service always left, but this was different, and as far as Reception was aware, no one had been into the room.

Surprisingly, this sort of thing had not happened to me much over the course of my career, and this was the first time I was certain of it. As unsettling as it was to know that my private effects had been tampered with, it was the first real confirmation that I was on the right track.

After packing swiftly and calling Jacobs from another payphone to warn him, I spent an hour or so travelling on the Underground, switching from train to train. Once I was convinced I wasn't being followed, I checked into a hotel in Earl's Court where I could pay in cash without ID. There was no formal reception area; I could just come and go through the narrow stairwell without being noticed. When I contacted Jacobs the next day he told me that he had managed to talk to the ex-staff member from the storage company, the unfortunate smoker. His name was Jim Dale, and Jacobs had arranged a visit for me – in Dale's company – to the Tate.

We met near the gallery the following morning. Getting into the building itself proved not to be a problem. There were two service entrances at the back on John Islip Street, an area I already knew, and they were manned by old-timers who appeared half-asleep. None of them were aware that Dale had been sacked, as he still had his security card, and he was able to arrange a day pass for me on the grounds that I was a security consultant at his company.

Once we were past the guards, there were several sets of reinforced doors which gave the place the air of a fortress; but in reality all that was needed to gain entry was a familiar face. From the entrance, a warren of windowless passages and stores led deep under the public galleries on the grid of the prison that had once stood there. There was no doubt in my mind that as a former employee and contractor, Bowen could have accessed this area at any time of the day or night. Each section was secured by doors with combination locks, so that once a person knew the numbers they could move freely throughout the area. It was not long before a picture had formed in my mind of Bowen having once inhabited these passages with all the familiarity of Gollum in his lair.

Dale had agreed to take me through all the places Bowen would have had access to, and we started in the loading bay. This was rather surprisingly not fitted with cameras, and the artworks stood about everywhere, covered in dust sheets and plastic. It did not seem as if it would have been difficult for other cargos to have arrived this way without attracting notice; nor for them to have been secured somewhere in the maze of storerooms, to be moved on later by the same route. Once past the guards, it seemed one could move about more or less unnoticed in these areas: art courier vans from the company were standing idle at the dock, their doors open, no one checking what they brought in or what they took out. They looked similar to the vans used by glaziers, and in the back were racks lined with rubber and felt where the artworks were strapped. The doors were air-sealed and the panels reinforced like those of bank security vans. It was difficult to imagine a safer way of transporting high-value loads – of any type.

I had made it clear to Dale that Bowen had been in possession of something of mine that I wanted back, and that we would not stop until we found it. Maybe there was something about my face that unnerved him as I said this, because all the time we were together he looked more than a little apprehensive. He behaved towards me as if I were someone of unsound mind who needed humouring. Moving on from the van dock, he showed me the office Bowen had sometimes used – which, like his rooms in Madrid, was a small, cell-like space. No doubt it had once formed part of the prison: the walls were of thick stone, the only light source an arrow slit onto a gloomy inner yard. We found nothing of interest there.

Around the office were many small stores, housing only cleaning supplies, display cases and lighting equipment used upstairs in the galleries. This led into a larger, less-frequented area known as the stacks; a maze within a maze, used to store the many pictures not displayed in the public galleries above. It was manned only by a single guard, and once past him we could move about undisturbed. Long railings were mounted on wheels so that they could be pulled out, and hanging on them were half-forgotten works rarely seen by the public. Briefly, in the gloom, ancient faces and landscapes reared up like images in a kaleidoscope before disappearing again. Beside these, along the walls, were deep cabinets in which prints and works on paper were kept.

We were down there for hours. We went through everything, feeling inside and examining the darker spaces with torches. In retrospect, it was both fortunate and surprising that no one even challenged us – a fired ex-employee, and a convicted drug smuggler whose face had been plastered all over the news for the last twelve months, rummaging around among priceless works of art apparently without let or hindrance.

By the end of the afternoon, it was evident that there was nothing to be found in the gallery. Still, it had been a useful insight into the world that Bowen had moved in. According to Dale, this left only one location operated by the museum to which Bowen would have had access: a warehouse in North London, used to hold works too bulky or otherwise unsuitable for public display. 'It's the Siberia of national art,' said Dale. This sounded promising. For security reasons, due to the value of its contents, the place was not featured on public maps – but Bowen, apparently, had sometimes gone there in a van alone. I was keen to explore it, but although Dale had been paid well for his services, he looked beat. I didn't want to push him too hard and risk losing him, so we agreed to leave the warehouse until he was next available.

I made my way back to the club feeling that after months of chasing shadows, I was finally making progress. Many of the decisions I've made in my life as a smuggler have been based on little more than gut instinct and experience; I had no real reason to believe that this time would be any different from the others. But, while I made sure to keep an eye out for anyone who looked as if they might be following me, I was in excellent spirits. For the first time in an age, I got a decent night's sleep.

14

Several mornings later, I met up with Jim Dale again. We made a few quick passes by the warehouse so that I could see what was involved. It looked like it was probably an Edwardian building, and it was definitely a strange one. From below it resembled a giant cricket pavilion, but from the front it was more like an old aerodrome hangar. The sides were windowless and made from rusting corrugated iron, and around it was a small industrial estate on the outer side of Acton. This was marked on our map as Gorst Road, though as Dale had indicated, the section of the store itself appeared blank.

The storage depot, Dale said, had been used to hold art during both world wars before the more valuable works were moved into salt mines and other underground locations. When I asked if he could recall Bowen having business at Heathrow cargo terminal, which was only half an hour's drive away, Dale wasn't sure. He was clearly more nervous than he had been at our previous meeting, and I tried my best to calm him down. I told him I would understand if he wanted to pull out, and not hold it against him; but he said he was all right. He asked me to drop him at the tube station, as he had an interview later that morning with another courier company.

'So – what sort of man was Bowen? What was he like?' I asked as we drove.

Dale seemed unsure how to answer. I don't know exactly what I was expecting him to say; perhaps just that Bowen had been one of the guys, or that he had kept himself to himself. Something banal that wouldn't affect my own image of the man. I waited. Finally Dale said, 'Just . . . fine.'

I pondered this reply. It was so vague, it could have meant almost anything: perhaps that Bowen was easy to get along with, and was never any trouble; perhaps just that he was a good worker who could be relied on; or all, or none, of these things. Dale seemed aware that he had not said enough, and I thought he might be about to elaborate – but we reached the tube and he left it at that, saying only, 'I need to be getting on. See you later?'

We agreed to meet back at the Gorst Road industrial estate that night, to look for residual traces of any drugs Bowen might have stored there.

The plan was to gain access to the warehouse using Dale's security pass, and sweep the premises with a sensor that I already had in hand from Jacobs. The sensor did not detect MDMA, but would easily pick up other precursor chemicals such as hexamine. Given the obvious size of the place, which was apparently used to store all the larger sculptures not on public display, this would save us the work of having to search each part by hand, as we had at the museum. As it would be dark, with the clock ticking, it seemed a safer option.

Jacobs had first got hold of the sensor device while reading a survey of air quality in haulage cabins in the course of pursuing one of his hobbies. He made regular use of it in smell-proofing consignments, and he was confident it could detect the relevant chemical precursors; it was used to check toxin levels in work environments, and was sensitive to about three parts per million of certain chemical vapours it came into contact with. But there were several ways to synthesize MDMA. Since Merck had used their own synthesis, and Shulgin had circumvented their patent by using another, kitchen and mafia chemists had improvised various routes to the same end. Ultimately, we were banking on Bowen having used hexamine as part of the process.

If the first sweep of the building, which would take a couple of hours, did not produce any readings, we intended to make a second sweep with a sniffer dog. We had one lined up with Mark Pullen, the associate of Dennis Watkins' – of whom, worryingly, there was still no news. It wasn't cheap – when a criminal obtained one of these dogs, he knew he had a valuable commodity and could

charge high rates to check the smell-proofing on drug consignments. The dogs normally lived with their police or
customs handlers, and took years to train. With noses up
to a thousand times more sensitive than ours, they could
detect smells over a mile away – even detect the smells of
objects that had been removed several months previously.
For the right dog, finding drugs was child's play. Using
them had its risks, though, as they had been known to run
amok and disappear.

In the event, my concerns about the dog proved well
founded. When we arrived, the dog – a springer spaniel,
who had been sitting quietly in the car – slipped its muzzle
and began barking. This brought the old guard out of his
cabin, looking none too pleased to have been disturbed.
It took Dale several minutes of waving his card around
to convince the man that he was there to deliver an art-
work before we were able to return to the business in
hand.

As planned, Dale then covered me in bubble wrap and
a velvet drape and trundled me in on a flatbed barrow,
disguised as a work of art. There were several minutes of
darkness and near-suffocation as we moved down the
gradual incline of the ramps. Below was a cavernous
space, with sculptures receding into the dimness on every
side. We passed the shadowy forms of Rodins lying on
their backs, the looming iron girders of Modernist pieces,
rake-thin Giacomettis peering from behind towering

Hepworths. Despite the value of the inventory, everything seemed to be stored in one big jumble together. It all had that dusty air of things left too long alone in the dark.

With the guard so near, it was too risky for me to wander around, so Dale pushed the cart between the rows while I worked the sensor over all the surfaces I could reach from beneath my drapery. Many of the works were hollow casts, and others had holes where plinths and stands had once been, so there were endless potential hiding places. As many of the works were solid steel and aluminium, it was difficult to know how far the sensor could penetrate. It struck me that if anything was properly wrapped within these spaces, we might not get readings at all; it was feeling increasingly like a fool's mission. This was confirmed when the sensor suddenly went off – much more loudly than we had expected – in one of the passageways, nowhere near any artworks or possible hiding places. It had been triggered not by hexamine, but by tubs of cleaning chemicals lined up against the wall there.

At this point, Dale ran for it, knocking over some of the cleaning equipment, which clattered appallingly and brought the guard out with his torch. When his footsteps began moving slowly towards the source of the sound, I lost my nerve in turn and hurled myself off the cart, plunging after Dale towards a smaller room at the back of the space. The guard was about twenty metres away when his beam of torchlight caught me.

I wasn't sure whether he could tell I was not Dale, but in these situations I've found it is often safest to act drunk. I began swaying about and calling back that I'd lost my way, then crouched down again. Whether or not he was convinced by this, the guard didn't come any nearer, but threw his hands up as if wondering what the world was coming to. I was aware that Dale was still hovering in the doorway behind me; if he broke cover, it would be obvious there were two of us, so I gestured back to him to keep down. My heart was racing. It had been a long time since I had been in a tight corner like this and I knew that if it ever came to court, with my track record, I could be locked away for a long time.

Dale was clearly far too scared now to contemplate bringing in the dog, but as the guard didn't seem interested in approaching us, we stayed put and hoped he wouldn't call for assistance. After a few minutes, I pulled myself together sufficiently to carry out a last quick search with the sensor. The room was filled with empty plinths and pedestals, almost all hollow, each with markings that presumably corresponded to one of the sculptures in the larger room. Some were made of hardwood, others of thin sheets of metal. Those designed to support larger works were reinforced with struts and bars, and as Dale lifted them I was able to work the sensor right up inside them. As I was no longer on the cart, I could even crawl in and get underneath some of them to check them manually. We had belatedly disabled the sensor's bleeper and were relying on its green-amber-red display.

After another twenty minutes of searching, I noticed a stronger signal coming from the other end of the space. The sensor started to turn to amber as we approached a row of high pedestals. A cluster of iron bars nearby fenced off what looked like a small dump of abandoned and broken plinths. It didn't look as if anyone had been in there for a while; rotten wood and catalogues for ancient exhibitions lay about in the dust. The sensor was briefly showing red, but when I picked the damaged plinths up I found nothing underneath. After turning everything over several times, feeling inside every plinth and piece of packing with mounting frustration, we found nothing more exciting than a few scraps of tape bearing the courier company's logo.

I straightened my back and blew out a long, silent breath. It suddenly felt as if we had been clambering around in this subterranean semi-darkness for hours, to no avail. Catching Dale's eye, I saw that he looked as discouraged as I was beginning to feel. If there had ever been something for us down here, it was now almost certainly gone, and the trail seemed as cold as the clutter of iron and steel that surrounded us.

15

It was well past time for me to reconnect with my family and, as autumn approached, I headed back to Mallorca for a short break. This time I kept a low profile, spent as much time as I could with the children and stayed clear of all the old drinking haunts that had previously sucked me back into my old lifestyle.

The Zurich scam that Drake had drawn me into was now about a month behind schedule. I still expected nothing but trouble to come from it; but finally we got the go-ahead to put the plan into action. I returned to the UK, and we held meetings in the cottages we had rented in Norfolk, going over all the details repeatedly to avoid any misunderstandings. Present were the three couriers Jacobs already worked with, and one other who was vouched for by Dennis Watkins' contact Mark Pullen, who I had already vetted. To be on the safe side, we were keeping Drake as far out of the picture as possible, but this did not appear to be a problem. In fact, it was notable how little communication there had been from him: normally a partner in a drugs deal is as anxious as anything and needs constant reassuring, but Drake seemed almost to have left the stage. This, like quite a few other aspects of the scam, did not feel entirely right to me.

Even though I'd had an uneasy feeling about the scam since the beginning, there were no solid grounds to call it off. At least six people were now depending on it and had invested their time in good faith – especially Jacobs – and I would have needed a good reason, not just a hunch, to pull the plug. With about £40,000 of my book royalties invested in the ski equipment we were using, and all the rental fees, and a net return of about £90,000 being anticipated, if Salomon paid at the promised rate, this was not the sort of money anyone was going to pass up. As things stood, all that could be done was for everyone to keep in almost hourly contact and watch everything like hawks. That way, if anything went wrong, most of the group would still have a chance to get loose.

After one final meeting in Norfolk, Jacobs flew to Zurich and moved the goods from the airport locker to an apartment in the Zoo Dolder district. Over the next few days the packing was done by the couriers, overseen by Jacobs; this way the couriers could be confident everything was done right. The powder for a million pills took up about three cubic feet when compressed, and half the load took up all the boots, jackets and ski cases already tested under the X-rays. The rest was kept back for a second run.

Arrangements had been made to bring a sniffer dog in from a German firm based in Hamburg to test the smell-proofing, but when they upped the price exorbitantly at the last minute, we made the decision that we'd have to make do with Jacobs' sensor – even though I had first-hand experience of its unreliability.

On the appointed day in the second week of December I took up position in a pub in King's Lynn, about half an hour's drive from the nearest cottage in Norfolk. Whenever Jacobs passed a public phone, he would ring in with an update. Everyone had pay-as-you-go mobiles, bought second-hand for cash just for that day, so they could either come through to me on those or from payphones en route. As the day progressed I stayed near the pub payphone, hogging it so that no one else could use it at times anyone might have called. I nervously worked my way through several pints and a whole packet of cigarettes as I waited for news from Jacobs on how the first leg of the scam was going.

We had chosen the busiest Sunday-night flight for returning skiers for the couriers to travel, so they would blend in. To ensure their safety, three decoys were seated at the front of the plane and were going through first. All they had to do was look as suspicious as possible to occupy the few customs officers on duty at that time of night. This was not going to be difficult, as they were the most low-down, bedraggled-looking types Mark Pullen had been able to recruit. Using decoys can be dangerous if they have any idea of the operation they are part of, but if they are made to think they have a small unrelated job to do, it is relatively safe. Pullen had given them each CD-ROMs, telling them they were carrying algorithms stolen from a Swiss company. There were indeed algorithms on the discs: anyone who tried to use them would be confronted with complete gibberish.

Finally, about four hours later, a call came through from Jacobs. The couriers had all got through safely to Gatwick and were on their way, travelling individually, to each of the cottages. It would now be my responsibility to turn the powder they were carrying into half a million pills, which Salomon and Purse would be selling on in the clubs of Ibiza as the clubbing season gathered momentum. Everything pointed to it being the biggest volume season yet.

One of the decoys, a student at Kingston College in London, had been busted with a small amount of hash on him which he had forgotten he was carrying. He had been questioned and released, but he had known nothing about the rest of the bigger operation. Still, to be on the safe side, Pullen decided to cut all ties with him. Nobody was unduly worried; Pullen was hardly known to the student, so if later the student's run was linked back to Pullen in some way, it was still unlikely to be connected to the rest of the operation. We moved swiftly on to the next stage.

Back home in Mallorca, 1996, less than two years after my release from Terre Haute on drug-smuggling charges.

'Just to look out of the window now and see the sunlight over the grass felt like a privilege, and gave me hope. The simple food my wife and daughters cooked – pasta, stews, paella – tasted extraordinary, like manna from heaven, and just to smell it mingling with the fresh air through the patio windows seemed the greatest luxury.' © Martyn Goodacre/Getty Images

A smiley face looks down over a crowd of clubbers in the mid-nineties. 'There were probably a couple of hundred partygoers present, some wearing the Smiley acid-face T-shirts and the music was loud.' © Matthew Smith / PYMCA / Rex Shutterstock

On the road promoting *Mr Nice*. 'As the summer of 1997 drew to a close, sales of the paperback of my book were reaching 1,000 copies per day.' © Tim Holt /Phatfotos

With Gruff Rhys from Super Furry Animals, Deia, Mallorca, 1996. © Martyn Goodacre/ Getty Images

Nicholas Saunders, drugs activist and author.
'His name was already known to me in connection with the popular *Alternative London* publications and the Neal's Yard health-food empire, both of which he had founded and of which he remained sole owner. The rumours I heard about him sounded far-fetched: it was said he had his own purity testing laboratory, and travelled around in a special van with an on-board lab, and that various European governments sent pills to him for analysis. Later, I would learn that all these rumours were true.' © Alex Lentati / *Evening Standard* / Rex Shutterstock

Summer 1997: flirting with Manumission girls in Ibiza.
© Howard Marks

Ibiza, summer 1998: Mike McKay and Claire Davies, the creators of Manumission, at the time the world's biggest nightclub. © Howard Marks

Manumission from above, Ibiza.
'One reason for Manumission's popularity was that it featured live sex acts involving dwarves, vampires and porn stars, which the audience were encouraged to participate in, and these guaranteed a heaving floor from about one in the morning onwards.' © PYMCA/Getty Images

Johnny Golden, Manumission's famous stage dwarf, and Derek Dahlarge, resident DJ at the Pink Pussy Motel. © Howard Marks

Raving with Russ Taylor of Fat Bloke Management, Manchester, 1997. © Howard Marks

Testing the purity of ecstasy, London, 1997. © PYMCA/ Getty Images

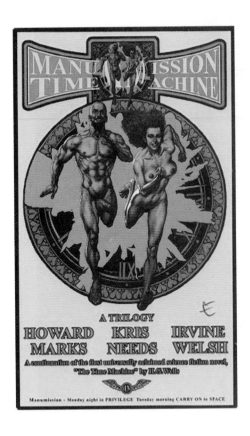

Above: **Ibiza, 1997.**
© Leelu/Getty Images

Opposite page, top: **Manumission poster, Ibiza, 1998.** © Howard Marks

Opposite page, bottom: **Nice 'n' Idle, 1998, at Fabric, DJing with Billy Idle.**
© Howard Marks

Left: **Wearing Brian Jones' Jalabiya and performing with the experimental hip hop group Islamic Diggers, London, 1997.**
© Howard Marks

Johnny Golden, Manumission dwarf, Ibiza, 1998. © Howard Marks

Stuart Cable (Stereophonics drummer, now deceased) and Rob Brydon, Cardiff, 2000. © Howard Marks

The greatest danger now lay in any surveillance placed on the four couriers themselves, as it was common practice for Customs to let couriers through and track them until they could wind up the rest of the ring. This was the reason I had insisted on four cottages – one for each of the couriers to make their drop – and over the next three weeks we would monitor these locations for any signs of surveillance. In the open fenland it was not difficult to see anyone approaching. Once we were satisfied the cottages were not attracting any attention, we brought in the pressing machine in several parts and checked it thoroughly for tracking devices. It appeared clean but was left in situ for another two weeks while we took turns watching the cottage, in case it had brought any heat with it. One of the ironies of this life – which my audience on tour rarely seemed to understand – is that for all the exotic associations smuggling carries, there is a huge amount of dead time spent simply waiting around.

The pressing took three days. The fine powder blew up through the cotton lab masks everyone wore and people began getting too high, wandering around like zombies to the point where the work rate slowed almost to a halt. Even Jacobs, normally so on the ball, was too high to work the controls properly and feed in the powder. To add to the mounting chaos, while we were mid-operation some locals turned up looking for a previous occupant of the cottage who apparently owed them money. I managed to get them to go away, but not until they had seen some of the rest of the gang through the windows, and they did not look impressed. When, a few minutes later, the postman arrived needing a signature on a package addressed to the owner of the cottage, there was a surge of panic in response to his ringing the bell. All the windows had to be flung open, and a lot of strong antioxidants taken, to get everyone's heads back in order and restore calm.

A further problem was that the logo Nick Salomon had supplied did not fit the head of the pressing machine which stamped it on. So much time had been lost by this stage that we decided to press the pills blank. This was a period when a lot of adulterated product was being sold under fake Mitsubishi and Calvin Klein logos, so I felt it did not matter much.

When everyone finally cleared off, the count was just shy of 500,000 pills – not bad, considering all the powder that had blown around. After taking an hour's rest, I called Salomon to give him the count and fill him in on the logo problem. He wanted me to meet Purse and do the drop that night, arguing that the less time I was in close proximity to the pills, the better. This seemed reasonable enough.

We arranged for the meet to happen in the car park of a nearby hotel. I was to deliver later that same evening, in person, as agreed. Purse was coming up from London, but as he lived in Cheyne Walk, only minutes from the heliport in Battersea, I didn't have to wait long. After a couple of hours, word came back that he was already at the meeting place.

I parked some distance away from the rendezvous point, to discourage anyone who might have thought about following me. Making my way slowly there, I could see Purse across the car park, sitting in a minicab with a grim expression on his face. The driver was nowhere to be seen. There was a bitter wind blowing over the fens, but Purse had the window open. He was staring out at me intently, as if I might suddenly disappear if he took his eyes off me for a moment.

He began talking in a general way, telling me that ecstasy dealers were often good at what they did, but tended to make poor businessmen. The way he presented it, it sounded like this could be a problem. Like most dealers, he said, they did not see themselves as dealers but as businessmen first and foremost. When they went into legitimate business, they almost always lost money hand over fist, only to feed their enterprises – clubs, restaurants, galleries or whatever their pet business was – with more dealing money: to fool themselves into thinking that they were really businessmen.

It was difficult not to wonder if Purse was really talking about himself when he said this, as he was known to own several prestige restaurants and galleries in central London. They all had high overheads which had to be fed in lean times. He also owned several international drink and beverage companies, among other legitimate concerns. But I had no idea whether these lost money, and as many big dealers owned such businesses, I tried not to make assumptions.

It was then that Purse – completely unprompted, which threw me – mentioned Bowen's name.

'But Henry Bowen. Now, *he* was something of an exceptional character.' He paused reflectively, and I tried not to show any reaction beyond polite interest.

'In what way?'

Purse waved a hand. 'Never made an investment – not beyond what he needed as a front for his operations. Bowen wasn't interested in being a businessman. He had principles, and he stuck to them. Gave a lot to charity. Last of a dying breed, he was.'

I nodded. It sounded plausible enough, given what Drake had already told me of Bowen's history. 'I'm sorry I never had the chance to meet him.'

All of this seemed, on the face of it, only a way of conveying that Bowen was someone with whom Purse had nothing in common. Purse's interest in Bowen was apparently simply explained: after Bowen's death, Purse had been contacted by the American buyer for Bowen's missing consignment. The buyer said he had already invested upfront, and he wanted Purse to recover what he had a stake in. This buyer was probably Juan Royal. Purse's relations with Royal had been rocky, going all the way back to the meeting in Barcelona in 1986 when Purse had hived off Ibiza; and now Purse wanted to mend fences with Royal, because the Balearic market was saturated. Ultimately, Purse's goal was to get into the States, where the serious profits were, and Royal still more or less controlled that territory.

As for Royal, I reckoned he had probably liked buying from Bowen because Bowen was the last of the peace-and-love merchants who still believed ecstasy could change the world. That meant it was a point of principle with him that his prices and quality were always good.

None of this explained where the missing stash was, but it all made so much sense that I almost believed it. When the driver reappeared across the parking lot and Purse tapped my hand to signal the meeting was over, I felt relieved. Perhaps Purse had wanted to see me only in order to deliver this message, and not go any further.

But there was another surprise to come. As I got out of the car, with the wind howling over the fens so loudly that I could hardly hear him, it sounded as if Purse was saying, 'But of course, Howard, we both know where the gear is.'

I must have looked baffled; I still had no idea. Purse stared at me, narrowing his eyes, as if I should know better than to play the innocent; but the driver had now reached the car, laden with cigarettes and sandwiches, ending the conversation. Purse said nothing more. The last thing I saw was him pushing the sandwiches under his seat and closing his eyes as the car moved off.

16

After all the weeks I'd spent preparing for the Zurich scam, I did some further shows in the Manchester area to meet demand. Before I knew it, the Christmas holiday period of 1998 was fast approaching. Much as I wanted to see my family, I knew it was safer not to return to Mallorca, where I could easily be tracked down; instead, I retreated back to the chalet near Estepona.

Purse had come good on his fairy-tale price, but after Drake and Jacobs had been taken care of, there had been almost no profit left in the scam for me, only a few miserable grand for all the effort gone into it. I found myself in low spirits, and I was in absolutely no hurry to move on to the second half of the goods still waiting in Zurich. I kept my head down, and the world beyond my chalet, trickling through to me via newspapers and conversations in bars, seemed very far away. As the news broke that Bill Clinton was likely to be impeached over the Monica Lewinsky sex scandal, I couldn't help but smile to myself: maybe he should have inhaled, after all.

The truth was that my options had become worryingly limited. Dope smuggling was now closed to me: I was just too visible, and no one would risk doing business with me. Most of my contacts were dead, retired, working as police informers or into other lines, and there was no longer a market for the quality product I had once sold. But doing straight work – like performing shows based on my auto-biography – was a lot of hard graft for very little reward. Writing took years to develop as a craft, and I did not think I had that sort of patience. I didn't know what to do with myself. Days of inactivity soon slipped into weeks. Fresh Moroccan resin and kiff could be bought from the boys at the beach, and most days I hung around the bar by the ruined *padel* courts, not doing much at all.

It was around this time that a new story about Bowen's demise reached me. The gossip around my local haunts had it that only weeks after Bowen's death, an aggressive Moroccan firm had found his gear, stepped on it and knocked it out for stupid money, bit by bit, into the South African market. This was a poor market to sell into price-wise, but it had the advantage of being out of the range of Purse and other interested parties. I wasn't sure I believed the story, but if there was any truth in it and Purse now knew about the Moroccans and intended to move against them, it only seemed like another good reason to keep out of his way.

Vague ideas about what my next move might be flitted

through my mind, but nothing ever seemed to stick. The only half-formed plan I kept circling back to was related to the area around Marbella, the area I had been drifting about in for so long. I felt it would be worthwhile to document the place in some way before it disappeared under the weight of all the construction work that was going on. This was hardly more than an idle daydream that kept playing in my head; but it was not surprising that the place was on my mind. For months, my enquiries about Bowen had taken me through most neighbourhoods – from the ritzy Puerto Banus and Golden Mile areas to the more mixed San Pedro de Alcántara, Estepona and Manilva strip developments, all along that same short stretch of coast which ran from Fuengirola in the east to Gibraltar in the west.

All these satellite communities were a few miles from the town of Marbella itself, and yet they were part of it. The town was not a sharply defined place with clear borders, but a loosely associated group of geographically separate areas, linked more by mood than by location. A village could be right next to the actual town and not be considered part of it, and yet by some alchemy a development twenty kilometres away was still considered 'within' it. Although I had visited Marbella often over the years, usually to meet associates in the marijuana trade, I had never really understood the place. Something about it had always mystified and unsettled me.

It had quite a reputation, of course, and was routinely referred to in the press as the capital of the so-called Costa del Crime. It was seen as a centre of money-laundering, strongly associated with criminal excesses of one sort or another. This had always seemed a good argument for not living there but in the more low-key Mallorca. But I knew enough now to understand these descriptions were clichés which bore little relation to reality. Some Marbella residents talked of what they called the 'cake effect'; as this was explained to me, the place had many layers, like a cake, and most of these layers never came into contact with each other. It was a town that had no one at its centre – that really had no centre at all.

My thoughts kept returning to the idea of making some record of the place for posterity, and in the process, trying to understand it a little better. I was wondering whether I would be up to making a documentary and launching a career for myself in the media. I had already done some brief snippets of presenting work for Channel Four during the previous year or two, and I was comfortable with having a camera pointed at me.

Partly as a way to further postpone the pressing of the remaining half-million pills, I called up a family friend, Sabrina Guinness, who was running a small studio in Ladbroke Grove in London. I hoped she might be able to get me some work. Sabrina ran a charity that kept local youth off the streets by training them in production skills, and she was able to put me in touch with an agent at International Creative Management called Joe Paulson. He handled A-list names like Julie Walters, Christopher Reeve and Nicholas Evans, author of *The Horse Whisperer*. It turned out that he was looking to independently produce a new project.

When I left a message at Paulson's office, he got back to me straight away. He seemed about the friendliest person I had ever spoken to. 'I've been dying to meet you for a long time, Howard,' he said warmly. 'I have huge admiration for all that you've done.'

My self-esteem, which had been dragging along the bottom, began swelling again, and though it was clear that Paulson had never visited the Costa del Sol and had only the vaguest idea where it was, that did not seem to put him off. The only thing he kept saying was that I needed to pitch him *harder*, but I didn't really understand. He said it with a mounting excitement that sounded almost erotic – 'Yes, yes, but harder, *pitch me harder*' – and I wondered if this was some sort of code I wasn't up on, or even a double entendre. 'I need you to get the essence of this project down in a half-page treatment for me – the *essence of the essence*, Howard, can you do that?' I agreed to do my best. But as I didn't yet have a particularly clear notion of the project myself, it wasn't going to be easy.

Paulson said he would call me back. A couple of weeks went by, and when I still hadn't heard from him I began pestering his assistant, Alison, who was as friendly as Paulson had been. During the pleasant conversations that followed, it emerged that Paulson knew my old smuggler friend Ed Miles from his time in Los Angeles. Of course, I was curious to hear how Miles had been doing – it had been over a decade since we'd last been in touch, and I was rather fond of him.

My impression was that Alison was rather proud of Paulson's association with Miles, and thought that any details she disclosed to me about Miles would reflect well on Paulson. Miles had apparently produced two major motion pictures, one of which had won several Oscars, and he was considered very much a Hollywood insider. He now collected modern art and lived among the stars in Malibu, with a view of the ocean. He was close friends with David Bowie and Iman, Rob Lowe, Robert Downey Jr and all the studio bosses. Alison seemed at pains only to say good things about him, and stressed how hard-working he was and how abstemious in his ways – so I was a little surprised when she mentioned that he was also a regular at the West Hollywood branch of Alcoholics Anonymous. Possibly sensing my surprise, she clarified that this was where all the deals were made and that all the power players attended as a matter of course.

It was difficult to tell, from what Alison had said, whether Miles had really reinvented himself or whether this was all an elaborate front for his old game. On the surface, his transformation seemed impressive, and yet some doubts lingered in my mind. After all (as I had learned to my cost), once you've known the quick-money rush of smuggling it is difficult to get it out of your system entirely, and the temptation to return is always there. When I checked Miles's credits, they were almost as impressive as Alison made out. The only thing I noticed was that he tended to be on the executive-producer end of the movie, rather than the creative side. Also, all his movies were independents, only partly financed by the big studios. It was possible he was using them as an investment vehicle for money made elsewhere; but of course this was pure speculation on my part.

A few days later, Paulson was in touch again. He still seemed full of enthusiasm about my loosely conceived Marbella documentary project and had several format ideas for me, one of which immediately caught my attention. It was not particularly original or profound, but I instantly knew it would work. Suddenly I could see the whole thing frame by frame in my mind's eye, and I got in my car straight away and drove out to see the locations we would use.

Paulson's idea was simple: in the late 1990s a certain type of alternative tour of Hollywood was becoming popular, in which out-of-work actors were taking groups around sites not on the usual tourist trail and giving them the lowdown. One of these, called the Murder Tour, took in the locations of famous murders and unexplained deaths. Now, I was to do something similar in the Marbella area: I would be filmed visiting notable underworld landmarks, explaining what had happened there. Paulson had suggested we have a bus full of actors playing tourists who would ask leading questions, with me standing at the front, dressed like a magical mystery tour guide; but I had ideas of my own about how it might work.

A number of high-profile events in recent underworld history had come to a head in the Marbella area, so many nearby locations were already familiar to the tabloid-reading public. People had long been used to seeing long-lens shots of Charlie Wilson, the Great Train Robber, wandering about looking dishevelled in the garden of his villa; or Ronnie Knight, Soho's 'Vice King', sipping drinks poolside; or Freddie Foreman, the Kray associate and East End godfather (who had come to my book launch, along with Brink's-Mat launderer Gordon Walker), whooping it up in any number of Costa bars. And lately the papers had run images of the blood left on the porch after Wilson and his dog were gunned down by persons unknown; of Ronnie Knight lying in a hospital bed after a savage attack by further persons unknown; and of Foreman being bundled unceremoniously across the airport tarmac to face a long sentence back in Britain. These pictures seemed, at first, to tell a story everyone thought they understood: that of the fall of the old order of the underworld as younger, more vicious criminals assumed their turf. But if you looked more closely, you'd find that the details of each of these well-known cases were very sketchy. No one knew exactly what had really happened – certainly not the press.

I planned to take Wilson's killing as my starting point, and from there follow a path that would end with the death of Henry Bowen. I could only hope that this project would get Bowen out of my system once and for all.

17

I spent the next couple of days taking photographs of three particular locations. They were all places I had visited in happier times – nondescript villas, like any others in the area. From behind their high walls peeped the usual roman tile roofs and bougainvillea. The lanes smelt of jasmine and honeysuckle, and it was difficult to imagine anything bad had ever happened there. The third day was spent at the public library in Marbella town collecting various photocopies of recent newspapers, which I took back to the study in the chalet, where there was an old Spanish chest the size of a coffin sitting under a window. This is where I started putting the details of the project together.

The pictures of the villas formed three clusters on the chest, and I linked them together with a piece of string. The first set showed the spot where, in April 1990, a man had waited for Charlie Wilson to come to the door and had then shot him – and his pet Alsatian – before riding off calmly down the hill on a yellow bicycle. The next showed a house where, five years later, the Essex drug lord

Pat Tate had sought refuge for a few weeks before his return to Britain – where his body had been found along with those of two associates, in a Range Rover in Essex woodland. The last showed one of the reputed hideouts of the gangster Kenny Noye, who at this time was Britain's most wanted man. Only three weeks before Paulson had suggested the project, Noye had been apprehended up the coast in the resort of Vejer. The previous year, the body of another former resident of the house (still unidentified) had been found on waste ground nearby. All these roads led back to the Brink's-Mat robbery, and the attempts to launder the gold through pills into Ibiza – all of which I had inadvertently found myself caught up in.

Beside the photographs of the three houses, I pinned four photocopied faces: Wilson, Tate, Noye and the unfortunate Unknown Man. I was developing a plausible theory about what linked these four men: if I was right, it was this link that explained the bloody trail which had run through the whole underworld for the last decade. At the bottom, I placed my postcard of the chalets at the Marbella Club, where Bowen had stayed. I didn't yet connect this to the other pictures with the thread, as there was no evidence at this stage to say his death had been part of the other events.

While I was staring at the pictures, another call came through from Paulson. He was back on the theme of *pitching hard*, and had set up conference calls with editors at the BBC and Granada. He gave me the times and numbers to call. 'We're going to pitch them where the sun don't shine!' he announced cheerfully, and I couldn't help laughing. He was also now proposing a complicated financing arrangement whereby the documentary would be funded by tax-break allowances from two British-registered companies he had previously done business with. He stressed that I should use only local film crews and editing people, so the real costs could be kept to a minimum.

At Paulson's suggestion I called at the offices of one of the local television stations, *Onda Zero*, off the main drag of Ricardo Soriano in Marbella. I explained what was involved, and the number of days' filming it would require. They gave me a list of charges per hour for different types of outside filming assignments: though the various categories made little sense to me, I faxed it back to Paulson, hoping it was what he wanted. That evening I sat in the study again and stared at the pictures of the three houses and the four men.

In my mind, it was clear enough how the killings were related. The first, the murder of Charlie Wilson, was one of those deaths that becomes almost iconic – a moment when something larger than a single man seemed to have died. Wilson had epitomized the macho old school of villains, the sort who were judged by their actions rather than their words; his life was the stuff of folklore. He had been treasurer of the Great Train Robbery gang, and after his arrest he had said absolutely nothing to the police, so was known as 'the silent man'. Within only four months of being sentenced, Wilson had escaped to Canada, then Copacabana, and he remained on the run for most of the sixties. By that time, beset by money troubles, he had slipped down into the more uncertain trades of money-laundering and middling drugs deals, and he was out of his depth. In the late eighties, he had been given several million pounds of the proceeds of the Brink's-Mat heist to launder into ecstasy, and the deal had gone badly wrong. Nobody knew exactly what had happened: either the drugs never materialized or, if they did, there was some-thing wrong with them. It was generally believed that Wilson was unable to repay his investors. He would have known the price to pay for that failure.

Below Wilson was the second cluster of photos on the chest, showing the house where Pat Tate had hidden before his murder in Essex woodland a few weeks later. Tate had been a hardman and minder who had graduated to run-ning the Essex ecstasy supply. At the time of his death, police discovered he had come back from visiting an air-strip used to bring in pills from abroad. Interestingly, the investment for purchasing the pills had again come from the Brink's-Mat proceeds, as Tate had been the heist gang's front man for investing their money into the currency of ecstasy; but again, it was not exactly clear what had gone wrong. There were suspicions that Tate, a known informer, had been talking to the police. Two other Essex men, Michael Steele and Jack Whomes, had finally been convicted of the murder; but though they had their own motives for disliking Tate, it seemed almost certain they had been acting on orders from elsewhere. There could have been a problem with the quality of the product Tate was supplying, or some of the product may not have materialized. Though no association with the Wilson death was made at the time, what was certain was that this killing, as in the Wilson death, involved the connection of ecstasy with Brink's-Mat money. While I now realized that I had stepped right in front of this moving train, I never really felt that I could suffer the same fate as these gangsters. I had always been lucky – or too small fry to be worth taking care of.

The third cluster of pictures related to more recent events: again, a nondescript villa and a face, this time of the Unknown Man. Here the story was less clear, but it seemed to bear the same hallmarks. In 1996 a former resident of the villa had been found dead in a shallow grave on wasteland nearby, and never positively identified, as was sometimes the case in gangland killings. All that was known was that he was an ecstasy middleman of some sort. He was remembered only by a series of aliases, his original identity and nationality never known.

What was interesting to me was that the house beside which the body had been found was one of a large portfolio of properties owned by the gangster Kenny Noye. It was no secret that these properties in Spain had been acquired by Noye from his role in the Brink's-Mat heist; Noye had been one of the chief architects of the smelting operation through which the vast proceeds had been laundered. It was Noye who had overseen the converting of those proceeds into ecstasy. Word was that the unfortunate middleman found nearby, like Charlie Wilson and Pat Tate, had some role in this operation, but this in itself did not explain his death. All one could say for certain was that it was unlikely Noye himself had anything to do with the death directly, as he would never have had the body dumped beside one of his houses. At the time it was found, badly decomposed, he had still been in Swaleside prison in Kent.

At the bottom of the chest was the postcard of the Marbella Club chalets where Bowen had stayed. Bowen's death had fallen chronologically in the series between Wilson's and Tate's, but of course it did not fit with the others. Bowen had not been a gangster, and his death had the appearance of an accident or possibly suicide; almost certainly, there had been no one else involved.

It struck me as unlikely that Bowen had ever bought gear from the mob, or supplied them knowingly or directly. He had been a hippie chemist, an idealist, someone trying to bring peace to the world; his friends had been bohemians and fringe society characters. It was difficult to think of a more different breed of man from those others who had died. On the face of it, the gangland pattern seemed to bring me no closer to Bowen. He may not even have known any of the other members of its bloody narrative. It looked as if we were dealing with two contiguous, but separate events. But I still suspected a connection.

18

Experience leads us to see patterns in everyday life – but a smuggler's life will teach you to beware of trying to predict events, and avoid making too many assumptions. A death that did not at first appear to be part of a series might, in fact, be integral to it. Everyone in the smuggling trade knew the killings taking place in the underworld for more than a decade had been connected in some way to the Brink's-Mat heist. But no one could be sure who was at the centre of it all or who stood to gain the most from these deaths.

If the Brink's-Mat gold had been sold directly to traders, its purity would have given its origins away, so it had to be smelted down and alloyed with lesser metals like copper and aluminium before it could safely be sold. The quantity was such that the material could only be sold off gradually, and as many routes to market as possible were used to spread the risk. Meanwhile, someone had to store it all, and twenty-six million pounds' worth of gold is not easy to hide. Some went to backstreet dealers, some through the Assay in Sheffield, some to reputable gold dealers, while the proceeds were invested in new apartments in Docklands, as well as a wing of Cheltenham Ladies' College, which had been sold to convert into flats, and in various small businesses in the East End.

It was notable that the killings had started from late '89, at the time when ecstasy had gone mainstream during the so-called Summer of Love. This was the point at which Kenny Noye had altered the direction of the laundering programme by turning the proceeds of the gold sales into the highly liquid asset that MDMA now comprised. His method must have appeared to have obvious advantages over traditional laundering routes: well-selected property might appreciate by 100 per cent over a five-year period, and business investments might return a few hundred, if one was lucky, but these investments were cumbersome and exposed to confiscation by the claw-backs of the judicial process. Ecstasy, on the other hand, reliably returned several thousand per cent of its costs of production and distribution, and it was a mobile, liquid, and virtually limitless resource.

In the years since '89, as the clubbing scene had taken off, Brink's-Mat money had flooded the British market as well as the Balearic and mainland Spanish markets with cheap ecstasy. But right from the start there had been problems. While still in Swaleside prison organizing a bulk shipment of ecstasy from Rotterdam, Noye was tipped off that he was the target of a major DEA and Drugs Squad surveillance operation that was closing in on him. Noye got out of the deal just in time. But the apparent bad luck kept on coming. The following year, Charlie Wilson, after setting up another large ecstasy deal on behalf of Brink's-Mat money, had been killed; then Noye himself, months after his release, was involved in a fatal stabbing incident on the M25 motorway in Essex. Though this was presented in the press as a road rage attack, from what I knew of Noye this was unlikely. Noye had acted as he had that day because after the death of Wilson, when Noye was confronted on the motorway, he had been afraid for his life.

And things had just kept getting worse for Noye. His minder and assistant while in Swaleside had been Pat Tate, and after his release Tate had been put in charge of Noye's ecstasy roll-out in Essex and East London. Throughout this time he was running sales through bouncers in a string of nightclubs, but within months of assuming these responsibilities he was on the run from death threats. Soon enough, he was found dead along with his two closest associates. It was some of Tate's ecstasy – bought from Raquel's Nightclub in Basildon, one of the clubs Tate ran – that had contributed to the death of Leah Betts, who died in late '95 shortly after her eighteenth birthday, having fallen into a coma soon after taking the drug. Up until this point ecstasy had been considered relatively safe, but this event had been reported in the press as the death of the age of its innocence, the end of an era.

Rave anthems like the Shamen's 'Ebeneezer Goode' were no longer charting; Britpop ruled the airwaves now, and the Criminal Justice Act of 1994 had outlawed raves. Some of the scene had moved underground again into the pay parties I had attended around London, and also into commercial super-clubs like Heaven and Ministry of Sound. The last of the idealism of the earlier years had all but evaporated; no one was even trying to hide that anymore. Only a little more than a year after the death of Leah Betts, the body of the unknown ecstasy dealer had been found near Noye's villa. As precarious a life as I had had as a dope smuggler, I had never been confronted by anything like this. Then, early in '98, Solly Nahome, a Hatton Garden diamond dealer who had been fronting Brink's-Mat proceeds to buy ecstasy, had been shot at close range by a motorcycle hit man, only for Noye himself finally to have been arrested after an anonymous tip-off just a few weeks before I began my research.

It was a convoluted story with no clear centre, but it reflected what had become of the mainstream drug trade in the few short years while I had been in prison. I wasn't going to begin pointing fingers as to who was responsible for all the carnage, but it was not difficult to see who had been the loser from Noye's Brink's-Mat roll-out. Some back-of-the-envelope calculations I made, based on club consumption and seasonally adjusted, showed that at the peak of his powers in the eighties Spencer Purse was bringing in about twenty million a year, net, from the British market. There would have been about the same amount from the Balearics and Spain, tax-free, and probably another five million from Germany and the rest of Europe. But by the end of the decade the situation had changed dramatically. The cheaper Brink's-Mat product had flooded the British club and rave scenes and the big clubs in Spain. Purse's share had shrunk from a virtual monopoly of about 80 per cent of both markets to only about 10 per cent, and for someone with over a dozen cash-hungry companies to run worldwide, this could not have been a comfortable change in fortunes. It seemed clear now that all these events led back to Spencer Purse – a fact that made me extremely uncomfortable about what the future might hold for me.

Though Purse had cast his net into new territories such as raves in Eastern Europe, Thailand and Hong Kong, prices were lower there and the volume could not compare to what he had known. This would have given him reason enough to team up with Bowen to break the US market, as it was clearly a matter of survival. To do this Purse obviously needed the cooperation of Juan Royal, and this in turn, for reasons I did not yet understand, seemed to rest on Purse resolving the Bowen matter.

As all this was spinning through my head, Joe Paulson

was on the phone again, and he was no longer talking about financing our documentary project through tax breaks. Now he was saying I needed to put together a two-minute show reel, which he wanted to use to sell territorial rights at a couple of forthcoming television sales fairs. Though this was not a business I really understood, I knew enough to feel that this was an unusual way of doing things. I was sure the sales fairs were used to sell finished products, which were shown at screenings – not to raise development money.

Paulson now wanted a storyline about how, in the sixties, Marbella had been a playboys' paradise – until the gangsters had come and ruined it, and made it a gangsters' paradise. About an hour later, he called back to tell me he had more good news: Robert Downey Jr had agreed to front the programme. To my knowledge, Robert Downey Jr had never even been to southern Spain, and knew nothing about the underworld. It seemed a bizarre decision to bring him in. But when I complained again, Paulson told me I had been *promoted* to executive producer, and faxed me a list of tasks and responsibilities.

I could have washed my hands of the project, of course, but I wasn't quite ready to let go of it yet. It felt like the time to take a step back and explore Marbella's so-called golden age – after all, who knew what I might find there?

19

The show reel was to be composed of establishing footage of various locations fashionable in the fifties and sixties, surviving nightclubs of that period, and Ava Gardner's former villa, which had apparently been a hub of the jet-set crowd of the era. These were to be accompanied by interviews with several 'legendary playboys of the golden age' and with closing contrasting shots of well-known gangster hangouts. Paulson's estimate was that at least four hours of real-time shooting would be required to make the two-minute reel. The voice-over by Downey Jr would be edited in at the end. The plan was to set everything up back to back, then bring in the crew at the last minute to avoid a lot of costly waiting about.

Paulson appeared to have done some research. He recommended I put a call through to the Marbella Club and ask for an interview with the manager, a certain Count Rudi von Schönburg, reputed to have been the main fixer for the jet-set crowd back in the day. I agreed, although I didn't expect much from this interview – the count was notoriously discreet about his former guests, even the dead ones, and the hotel had the reputation of being one of the most tight-lipped in the world. Presumably this was why Bowen had used it as a base.

While waiting to hear back from the hotel, my next day was spent looking for Ava Gardner's villa. All anyone seemed to know was that it had been on the east side of town, in the Los Monteros area. This had once obviously been a charming and untouched stretch of the coast, with sandy pine hills stretching down to a small working fishing port where one could buy catches fresh on the quays and while away the day eating *mariscos* and *gambas* in the cafes. Alas, little of that charm remained, as the hills had been built over with high-rises and golf condominiums. No one there had even heard of Ava Gardner. As it seemed unlikely that many people actually knew what her villa looked like, in some desperation my search widened to any plausible-looking villa from the forties or fifties. All the villas looked a lot newer than that, the sort of closed-up compounds shut for most of the year behind high walls, with security warnings on the gates and dogs that barked before you even got out of the car.

The next location on Paulson's list was a nightclub called Pepe Moreno's that had apparently been a centre of playboy high-jinks. I had some rather faint memories of the place from the mid-seventies, but it had been closed for many years. The old building stood beside a busy new highway leading out from the main drag of Ricardo Soriano towards the Golden Mile. It was difficult to think of a less photogenic place: on one side was a Burger King, and on the other a long concrete strip. Some boys with slicked-back hair and chains in their back pockets immediately came up and asked me what I was looking for. Maybe it was just a helpful neighbourhood.

Easing my way through the hedge enabled me to take photographs through the dusty windows of the club, but not much remained inside; the room that would have been the dance-floor had an olive tree growing through the middle of it. This had been there in the old days, and I remembered sitting under it once with the racing driver James Hunt, who had owned a club round the corner called Oscar's. A vague memory came back to me of asking him why he wasn't hosting at the club, to which he had replied that his door staff had banned him from his own place for bad behaviour.

I repeated this story to the count the following day, when he was able to see me at the Marbella Club, in the hope that he would reciprocate with similar stories and provide material. I was wearing my best linen suit, in an attempt to look like the sort of person he was accustomed to dealing with. After I passed muster with the women at the front desk, who all looked as if they had graduated from Swiss finishing schools, the count met me in person and walked me down through the tropical gardens to the pool area, which overlooked a quiet beach. The way wound past glimpses of the private chalets from my post-card to where a large buffet was laid out under awnings, but there was hardly anyone about.

Seeing my attention straying towards the chalets, but obviously protective of the privacy of his guests, the count steered me over to the buffet. As I filled him in on the project he seemed interested and helpful, but when I asked anything specific, he would only say apologetically, 'I'm afraid I don't recall. Such a long time ago, you know.' The only playboys of the golden age I thought might still be around in the vicinity were Stewart Granger and Don Jaime de Mora, the latter a Spanish aristocrat and pianist who had squired some of the beauties of his day; but the count shook his head sadly at the mention of their names. 'Both quite dead, I'm afraid.'

As I tried to ask more questions his wife, Princess Marie-Louise of Prussia, conveniently appeared with an offer to show me round the gardens. This was no doubt a practised deflection strategy, but it was so graciously done that it was difficult not to go along with it. The princess was rather less intimidating than her name suggested, a cuddly-looking blonde with the kindest eyes I have ever seen, and they both walked me down the winding paths between the palms and yucca and other tropical plants, telling me the Latin names of every bush and where it had come from and when exactly it had been planted. It was difficult not to feel the place work its magic on me. I remembered the story about how the hotel had once just been a private house, but the guests who visited had been so entranced by the beauty of the gardens that they had stayed on for months, like lotus-eaters, and so gradually the place had evolved into a hotel by necessity.

As if to illustrate the point, there were lotus flowers of various sorts along the path at the edges of ponds and small brooks which led down to one of the small chalets just above the beach. Its terrace was ridged by guava and papaya trees, and the only sounds were the croaking of frogs and soft, distant piano music. The air was filled with the scents of blossom from the sea pines and jasmine and orange trees, and in the dusk the colours were more subtle and varied than any painting of paradise I had ever seen. Bougainvillea cascaded over the walls and mingled with ferns and flowers from the tropics. The count instructed me that there were over thirty types of bougainvillea in that place alone. 'Each has been chosen to complement the others in scent and colour,' he explained proudly. A fascinating fact, but not exactly what I had come here in search of. Half-hidden by the foliage, the chalet we were approaching was called La Paz – 'the Peaceful One' – and I knew instinctively that this was where Bowen had stayed. I could sense that the count and princess got wind of my heightened excitement.

Near its door was a row of lime trees, apparently planted to provide for the first dry martini of the evening for the Duke of Windsor, who had always stayed there. No doubt many guests had been taken on the same path before me and heard that same story, but it was delivered in such a way that one felt it was being told for the first time. Walking back through the gardens, the count divulged a few similar stories about the old times, but these were just a standard repertoire, already familiar to the public. His legendary discretion remained intact, and my efforts to wheedle leads to other people from that time who might talk came to nothing.

In the end, all I came away with were some old photographs of parties at the hotel from the forties and fifties: most of the names meant nothing to me, though in among all the forgotten faces were some that seemed recognizable. There was one that looked like Audrey Hepburn, a girl with short spiky hair sitting on a swing near the same wall covered with bougainvillea. Despite the forty years that had passed, the spot was curiously unchanged. Another showed someone who was surely a young Edward Kennedy outside the same chalet; others showed aristocrats and socialites of the same period, forgotten figures like the Countess of La Rochefoucauld and the actor Mel Ferrer, wandering through the same gardens.

A few old photographs were clearly not going to make

a show reel, and I drove around for several more days, determinedly looking for other traces of the old order. The post-war buildings had mostly been redeveloped, especially along the shoreline, and predictably the older villas, which had once stood in large grounds, had been built over with apartment blocks. The old estates in the hills were now mostly golf clubs and retirement communities. Despite all these physical changes, what struck me was that the town hadn't really changed much in terms of its core purpose. The first urban development had been built in '44 by a follower of General Franco, to accommodate fleeing Germans in the aftermath of the Nazi collapse. The Marbella Club had also first been built as a refuge, a hideaway from the post-war mess. The town had been a series of boltholes since its beginning. That was why the oldest villas tended to have the highest walls.

It struck me that the dope smugglers and gangsters like Foreman and Wilson were, in fact, just continuing an older tradition when they settled in the area. This might not fit Paulson's narrative of paradise destroyed, but it confounded expectations in a way that was perhaps more interesting. Though I knew they might not amount to much in his terms, I passed my thoughts on to Paulson along with a few of the old photographs. By this point, though, I was beginning to feel it hardly mattered whether the project got off the ground – the possibility alone had provided me with something to focus on, and delving into the history of the area had helped me to see more recent events in a new way. Soon, though, I would have more pressing present-day problems of my own to deal with.

20

For several weeks afterwards I did not hear back from Paulson, and by the spring of '99 I assumed that he must have lost interest in the project. The last I'd heard from him, he had shifted location to Monaco to secure a co-production deal from the French television channel Canal Plus. There was talk about using a French actor, Daniel Auteuil, as the front man. Paulson was still making me promises, but I had moved on mentally by this stage and no longer bothered to call his assistant for updates.

As things quietened down again I remained at the chalet and continued with a few more dilatory enquiries about Bowen, but I was now resigned to their not leading anywhere. For a brief period I found myself effectively treading water, waiting for something to happen. Idleness has always tended to have unproductive effects on my mind, and soon my actions would be directed primarily by fear and the desire to keep hiding.

One evening, I drove from the chalet to a bar between Mistral Beach and Pedro's Beach, about a hundred metres west of Banus. It was not one of my usual haunts, but I was tired of the indifferent quality of the Moroccan dope being sold near the chalet. I had a lead to a guy selling genuine Pakistani, and wanted to see if I could scout out some more.

Recently this area has been taken over by swanky outfits charging fifty euros just to use a lounger, but at this time it was still low-key. There were just a few shacks with scruffy palm roofs, selling beers and cold drinks. The season hadn't started yet and in the evenings there was hardly anyone about. As I did not find whoever I was looking for, after a couple of drinks I drove up to a *cortijo* which had recently been converted into a restaurant, about ten kilometres inland near the village of Istan.

After this detour I drove back home, slowly at first, the lights on full beam; I needed to concentrate so as not to miss the turnings. The road was little more than a track in places, and looked like all the other tracks branching off into the abandoned olive terraces. As I followed the path made by the ruts of the site trucks past the entrance to excavations made by the company that owned the land, the flooding left by recent rains made it difficult to judge the forks. I was becoming more aware of a putrid smell which seemed to have been with me since I had set out; at first I'd thought it must be some forgotten shopping in the back of the car that had gone off. But as I came down into the last hills above the coastal plain, the road leading

along the edges of more ploughed-up abandoned olive terraces, the smell persisted, growing stronger. I began to
wonder if a dead mouse or lizard had been caught in one
of the air vents. I opened the windows, trying not to gag.

At the bottom of the hill I stopped and checked. The
smell seemed to be coming from the outside of the car,
through the rubber around the boot. It was slightly tacky,
as if that part had been stained with something, but in the
evening darkness I couldn't make out its colour or consis-
tency. There were few lights along this part of the road,
and most of the rest of the way would be dark also, so I
would have to wait to see what it was.

At the beachside the shops and bars were still mostly
closed for winter. The only people visible were small hud-
dles of Filipinos and staff from the larger villas, waiting on
the irregular bus service. In minutes, I had covered the
stretch of highway beyond Las Dunas, lined with new,
largely unsold condominiums, and at the one battered sign
for Valle Romano, turned right onto the potholed slope
that led to my chalet. From above, it appeared to be set in
extensive grounds, but this was an illusion. The villas to
either side were vacant shells, never lit up, and all around
were the dark flanks of the overgrown links. I was in the
habit of leaving the car there, a little way down the lane
where it was shadier. The steps to the door were not evenly
spaced and I kept having to look down, watching my footing over the half-buried bricks. As my eyes came up again

to the level of the lane, I could make out a shape hanging in the eucalyptus tree over my parking place.

I went back to take a closer look, but in the half-light, the shape was no clearer than it had been at the door. Standing on the bonnet, trying to pull the thing down, I could see now that it was a dog which had been partially skinned. From its sharp, pointy nose it looked like a *podenco*, one of the short-haired, knee-high hunting dogs used in the autumn when bands of men came up the valley to shoot the rabbits that flourished there. Dogs that were gun-shy or poor of smell would often be abandoned at the end of the hunt and could be glimpsed through the winter, emaciated and nervous, foraging in the bins along the track.

I felt uneasy. For weeks, I had seen no one near the house – and yet someone had gone to the trouble of coming to the end of the lane, a cul-de-sac which led nowhere, and hoisted the thing up into the tree. There were many other trees they could have used, easier to reach, but they had chosen the one I always parked under. Whatever the message, and whoever it was from, I knew that it was meant for me; and much as I liked to see the best in things, a dog hanging outside the house did not strike me as a friendly gesture. Someone clearly thought that I was prying too closely into their business. I could see no one along the lane, and the slope of scrub above was, as usual, still and silent.

The dog's paws hadn't been denuded of skin, so I used them to pull the whole carcass into a blanket I had in the car, and took it inside to look at it more closely. The body was rigid but light, which suggested the dog had not been eating much in its final months; but the smell of decay was heavy. I wondered now if putrid liquid from the animal had dribbled down onto the car and been responsible for the similar smell I'd experienced on the road. The odour was filling the house, so I pulled the carcass into the laundry area at the back which housed the two chest freezers. In the light, it looked an odd sort of dog: short in the body, as if bred from an abbreviated pointer. Many of the local sanctuaries would not take this breed in, as the animals had a reputation for being destructive and digging up the plants in gardens. I had never seen one close up before. Under the bright bulbs, on the bare concrete floor, its body looked more frail than it had when hanging from the tree. The peeled skin barely covered the thin strips of flesh on the bones, and where the eyes had been were two just dry slits, the eyeballs perhaps picked away by birds, its fur there thin and matted black.

The freezer was empty. I lowered the bundle in, switching on the unit at the mains, and closed the lid tightly. Outside the laundry room was a hollow under the rain tank where I planned to bury it later, deep enough that the other valley dogs couldn't get to it; but my plan was to store it for the moment, in case there was a need to examine it again. The dog was a hunter, and I had been hunting after a fashion in my enquiries about Bowen. Was this to be my fate also, if I continued hunting? To be flayed and strung up, my eyes gone? In my heightened state, this seemed to be the obvious message. I had never been easily scared, but now, for the first time, I genuinely feared for my life.

My thoughts turned to Nicholas Saunders – dead, killed in an ambiguous car accident at the time I had contacted him for information about Bowen – and to Elisabeth Dermot and Dennis Watkins, my other two sources on Bowen. They were both still missing, and I hadn't heard from either over the last year. Although I had no solid proof, I became convinced that my life was in imminent danger. The following week, my instinct would be proved correct.

I had planned to see an old Gibraltarian friend, a former hippie and retired hashish smuggler who had changed his name several times over the years and was now known as Winston Smith (a nod not to George Orwell's *Nineteen Eighty-Four*, but to his former side-line as a cigarette runner from tax-free Gibraltar into mainland Spain). He had changed his name because his real name, Joe Bosano, was the same as that of an unpopular and maladroit local politician. However, I still called him Bosano, as it was a nice reminder of the good old days when life had seemed – especially given the current state of play – much less complicated. Our plan was to have some drinks at the same beach bar west of Banus where I had been the previous week.

Bosano looked tired and preoccupied; the bright eyes I remembered from the old days were as clouded over with worries as my own had become latterly. While he was less expansive than his usual self, I had the sense his business interests were not going well. We went in Bosano's Land Cruiser, as I still couldn't get the smell of dead dog out of my car despite thorough attempts to clean it. Bosano's car, on the other hand, was immaculate and smelt as if it had just left the showroom. In half the time it had taken me to cover the same distance, we had come down to the coast road.

I wanted first to get his thoughts on the dog in the tree, and as we passed the first of the unfinished apartment blocks, I told him that I'd heard about a similar dog being found near the house of some friends. Glancing up, as if at the flickering outline of the hills, he told me that back in the seventies there had been a wealthy Arab family up in Madroñal who kept exotic pets, including several panthers. After the head of the family – the well-known international arms dealer Adnan Khashoggi, rumoured to have supplied both sides during the Arab–Israeli Six Days War and the Yom Kippur conflicts of 1973 – had been detained in New York, the clan had disappeared overnight. The animals had broken out of their cages and begun roaming the countryside, picking off goats and domestic pets. They were said to have been breeding in the wild for decades. Bosano gestured with an open palm towards the band of darkness on the hills that marked the area of secluded multi-million-dollar estates around Madroñal, as if to say that up there, anything was possible.

The story sounded like an urban myth, reminding me of rumours about wolverines and wildcats that would circulate in South Wales whenever local farmers found any sheep ravaged. I wasn't convinced it was an avenue worth pursuing, but I asked Bosano if he'd heard of any local village rituals involving dogs in this way. I had heard a lot of stories since I had moved here about animals being tortured during such rituals: donkeys thrown off steeples, dogs having firecrackers attached to them and the like. But Bosano was already shaking his head, and looking ahead to where the road ran on beyond the lights of the Kempinski Hotel. The plain there was a patchwork of untended bamboo groves built over with villa complexes and campsites that did little business out of season. Bosano suggested that a more likely explanation was the local trade in fighting dogs. It made sense, I thought, that in a country in which bullfighting still attracted its Sunday crowds of aficionados, there should still be a taste for dog fights; but it seemed unlikely a trainer would have chosen to drive all the way up to my lane for the sole purpose of suspending an emaciated reject from a tree.

We drove on in silence, past the strips of closed-up shops and empty apartments, until we reached a turn-off hidden by a huddle of uprooted palms and builders' rubble. The place was easy to miss. The way down was blocked by more rubble, and further on were a couple of ruined villas which were used as parking lots in the season. At the bottom the track narrowed under the walls of the beachside compounds. Sand had blown across the track, and when we parked we found the path ahead to the bar had disappeared under a coarse, dark mud.

At the end of the track, just visible through the palms, was the vague, unlit outline of a villa that had once been owned by Sean Connery and his wife Micheline. The place had been closed up for years after a legal dispute over its proximity to the beach. Much of the sand under the villa's high wall had been washed away by the recent rains, and each summer convoys of flatbed trucks from the municipality, laden with sand from more sheltered beaches, would come to replace what had been lost during the winter months. Where the sand was washed away, there was the smell of outflows coming down from the hotels. Avoiding these, Bosano led me up some rough wooden steps towards the wooden beach bar known as a *chiringuito*.

These bars could be found on most beaches on the coast, their clapboard exteriors looking golden in the sunlight but grey and unwelcoming in the winter. Only its

location, next to Banus, lent this place the small appeal
that it had. Along the walls were dim booths, banquettes
that all looked empty, and around them strings of old balloons that sagged down like udders; the main cabin was
decorated in the style of a thousand run-down diners, with
battered American number plates fixed to the walls alongside whisky mirrors and faded posters of Marilyn Monroe
and James Dean. Despite the cool weather, the men at the
bar were wearing shorts and polo shirts, and they looked
like tennis instructors or crew off one of the yachts in
Banus who had come down to the beach looking for a
quieter watering hole than the clip joints on the strip. The
glossy older blonde women they were chatting to all had
the facsimile Marbella look: hair cut straight, just short of
shoulder-length, deep spray tans, plenty of fat gold jewellery. They could have been rich divorcees down from
Sierra Blanca or Madroñal, but I put them in the middle
ranks of the small army of therapists, trainers, stylists,
beauticians and decorators who serviced Marbella's retired
rich, and who were increasingly difficult to tell apart from
their employers.

Two of the tables had been joined together and laid
with jugs of sangria and *tintoverano*, and two of the
blonde women were slow-dancing together. Close up, with
her heavy make-up and tattooed lip and eye lines, the
waitress who came over to take our order looked like a
parody of femininity, and I wondered if maybe this was

why Bosano liked the place and had insisted we come here. Looking around at the uneventful scene, I couldn't think of any other reason why a man of his proclivities would, but as the dealer with the good Pakistani frequented the place, I was not going to protest.

He talked on, in an unfocused way, about other potential dog-killers along the coast. He thought mature male baboons were also in the frame, and seemed to be trying to put my mind at rest: he told me the source of the baboons was a forest called Piña del Rey, near the border with Gibraltar, a favourite weekend destination for Gibraltarians during the spring and autumn. Because they lived so close together on the Rock, the inhabitants loved the peace and space up there. In the seventies the Rock's authorities had planned a nature reserve to attract tourists and introduced green parrots and baboons to the area, but some of the animals had broken out, and also lived wild in the hills.

Bosano didn't look amused, or particularly engaged with any of this, smoking his tax-free cigarettes in shallow puffs and coughing throughout. Still, by the end of the evening he had almost persuaded me that the dog was nothing to be concerned about, most probably a prank by nasty kids. Not without a certain logic, he reminded me that anyone worth worrying about would have used more direct means and not resorted to such theatrical gestures.

Then, casually, as we were finishing our drinks, he dropped a bombshell.

'You know Salomon and his men have been looking for you around here? What's that about?'

I nearly choked on my beer. 'Looking for me? Where? Saying what?'

'Doing the rounds of the bars, asking for your address. Offering money. Sorry, man, I assumed you knew they were hanging around.'

'Christ.' Salomon had my number, so their wanting my address could only suggest they wanted to catch me unawares. Maybe there were innocent reasons for their interest in where I lived, but for the life of me, I could only think of troubling ones.

By now, the bass on the music was cranked up so loud the glasses and ashtrays were vibrating on the table tops, and I could hardly hear what Bosano was saying. One of the blondes was lying on her back among the empty jugs of *tintoverano*, her friend standing over her pouring from a vodka bottle, the others crowding in to lick up body hits. Bosano raised his hand, calling the waitress to bring over the tab.

We drove back to the chalet, but now there was a car parked up the lane. Two men I didn't recognize were sitting in it, and the lights were off. Suspecting they were Purse's men, the same ones who had been looking for me, and not wanting to risk stopping to pick anything up, I got straight into my car and drove off as quickly as I could. I continued to the highway past Estepona, where traffic was light and I could be sure no one was following. I picked up some toiletries and a change of clothes at a service station, and at the Manilva turn-off, I made towards Gaucín and the national park below the Serranía de Ronda.

The first stage of my plan was simple: I intended to stop at Antar's and give him a cock and bull story about where I was heading. A lot of faces had seen me with him at Dreamers and La Notte. I reckoned it wouldn't be long before Salomon and Purse were knocking at his door, and with luck this would put them off the scent. I could only hope that they hadn't gone there already.

21

The narrow road up to Gaucín rose between the sheer jagged bluffs which had made it one of the last Moorish strongholds to fall to the Catholic Monarchs. It had also been used during the Civil War to repel Franco's invading army of Moroccan mercenaries. Stories still went around town of how old Moroccan families in the Atlas kept the keys to their ancestral homes, and took secret and solemn oaths to return one day, but in the darkness it was not possible to make out the town or anything much ahead. Halfway up, after what felt like a week on the run, I was so crushed by tiredness that I had to pull over to rest.

Purse had given me a warning in Norfolk – to stay away from the Bowen matter – and now, it seemed, he was acting on it. Perhaps he felt he had told me too much at our meeting and that I had now become a liability; or perhaps with the story about the Moroccans taking the gear going round he felt embarrassed that the situation was out of his control. As he had been shown up in front of Juan Royal, he needed to reassert his authority. In any case, I knew that in these situations it did not really matter why someone was after you. Once the search was on, it took on a momentum of its own.

A little later Bosano called my mobile. He had returned home to find Salomon's henchmen waiting, wanting to know where I was, and they had only left after giving him some rough treatment. I was clearly a wanted man. As he was one of the few people I had been seen around with, this turn of events wasn't surprising; but what he went on to say was something I hadn't anticipated.

After the visit, Bosano had called Salomon to try to smooth things out. The story that transpired was stranger than I could ever have imagined. Salomon had told him the gear I had sold them from Drake had not come from India, but was part of Bowen's stash – a small part, probably only about a twentieth of it. As Drake was nowhere to be found, I was now their main lead.

Even with all my years of experience as a smuggler, it was a struggle to take in all the implications of this, but, if accurate, that made the total stash about twenty million pills, a number that was difficult to ignore. Although there had been bigger scams, I suspected there had been few on this scale of such apparent purity. Of course, Drake and Bowen were old friends. I had assumed their friendship was long in the past, but apparently I had been wrong; in which case, Drake's and Purse's odd behaviour made a lot more sense. I thought back to all that time spent chasing my tail, hiding from security guards in sculpture warehouses, while it now looked as if the Bowen stash, at least a part of it, had been in my hands all along.

It was difficult to rest now I knew this, though I badly needed to. Out in the dimness, I could just see the upper parts of the Manilva wind farm, built high on the bluffs to catch the Atlantic westerlies. I could have chosen a better place to stop: it was said in the bars of Banus that one night, while the site was under construction, some drunken stags had slipped their groom a Mickey Finn. He had ended up strapped to one of the vast propellers. A few minutes later a wind had got up and the thing began to turn, the g-force crushing him and distributing his body over a kilometre radius.

More urban myths, I hoped; and yet, my nostrils seemed to be catching some sickly-sweet odour coming from out on the hillside. Edging the car higher up, where the only smell was that of the night flowers, I looked out at the lights of Manilva and other resorts spread below along the coastal plain. At first sight, it seemed a fertile environment to hide in: off-season there were dozens of hotels which would offer rooms for cash, no questions asked. The trouble was that Purse would know this, as he would know about my house in La Vileta, so there was no point in going back there and putting my family at risk. Down on the coast, hundreds of holiday apartments were also advertised in *Sur* and the other English-language papers, and many owners would not be choosy about seeing the credentials of their tenants if the right amount of cash was fronted. In the worst-case scenario, Purse could potentially work his way through all the ads and lettings agents within a few days. So my preference was for something not advertised in any form. As many concierges and *porteros* of blocks offered an informal letting service to supplement their incomes, it was a matter of finding the right area and making enquiries. As in most resorts, people were coming and going all the time, so even off-season a new face hopefully wouldn't stand out too much; particularly if I stayed mostly indoors until the heat had passed.

I must have fallen asleep for several hours, because when I awoke it was already daylight, and with some trepidation I continued upwards towards Antar's. The familiar sharp outlines of the hills were blurred by the dust blowing in on the wind across the straits. The dark rectangle of the forest, where the cabin lay, was covered in a fine reddish mist, blotting out the cubes of the houses and hanging low over the ridges so that the whole landscape had the glaze of something seen on waking from a long sleep. When I finally reached Gaucín the sand wind was still blowing, and with visibility on the road down to no more than a few metres, it took almost an hour before I reached the turn-off into the forest.

The road ran along a steep river valley, through closely planted groves separated at intervals by harvest trails and fire breaks; it was marked by occasional wooden signs and used only by bark trucks and traffic to the few farms. Along the last three kilometres the way led between trees that were older, more spaced apart, no longer planted in grove lines, the trail running along rock-bedded ridges and outcrops. In the dry season the sky here would be filled with the circling of hawks and buzzards, crossing from the Moroccan mountains to pass the summer months in the cool of the sierra, but now all but the highest of the saw-edge peaks were invisible behind the low reddish clouds.

Through the cork and carob trees, on the left side of the track, I could now see glimpses of the half-submerged cabin. The camouflage netting was still there, but no rusting Land Cruiser, and as I parked some distance away and approached cautiously, I had the impression the place was locked up. Going closer, I saw that most of the photographs and other things I had seen inside on my earlier visits had gone. It looked as if no one had been there for a long time.

I left a message conspicuously on the door, saying I was going to Pakistan for a few weeks. In reality, I did not want to risk going anywhere near an airport, as most in the region were small and it was easy to be spotted; but I hoped this would at least draw some of Purse's people in the wrong direction. As I left, visibility through the mist became so bad that I lost my way: instead of coming out at Gaucín, the track had taken me to a place where bark was stored. As I tried to turn, the windscreen kept clogging up with dust, the wipers sticking.

Then my phone rang. I realized I must have switched it on again by mistake, and Salomon came on the line, saying he knew where I was. He tried to sound threatening, but I was not convinced: after all, I didn't know where I was myself. I could hardly see more than a few metres ahead, so it seemed unlikely anyone else could see me either.

Hanging up, I found my way back to the Gaucín road. Satisfied that Salomon had been bluffing and there was no one following, I stuck to my original plan. Once back on the coast I drove around the backstreets of the resort town of Torremolinos, looking for a suitable bolthole. I found a block of flats a couple of streets back from the old bus station, known as the Portillo, in an area where immigrant workers waited for cash building jobs and a few street girls operated. I liked the building because it had shops on the lower floors, did not look at all residential, and was the sort of place one could easily pass by and not notice.

The porter was an elderly local gentleman, sitting in a glassed-in cubicle filled with images of saints and old lottery tickets. He looked bemused at my request, clearly not used to anyone being interested in the place, but he showed me flat after flat, all empty and almost identical. The one I chose was high up, with a view down to the building's access points, and I paid him a few weeks in advance, and a tip to let me know if anyone came round asking questions about me. Then from the Supersol along the street I bought several weeks' supply of water and tinned goods, and some books and videos from the second-hand shop on the same road; I also stocked up on some Moroccan resin at the Portillo. It seemed unlikely I would need to venture outside the safety of the block now for a while.

The next few days passed in a blur. I left my phone off most of the time. Apart from a few messages from my management company in London about forthcoming dates for the show based on my autobiography, and a couple of requests to judge cannabis competitions, the world seemed to be leaving me alone. I left a message for Jacobs telling him the second half of the Zurich deal was on hold until further notice. A couple of hours later, there was a message back from Jacobs saying that Drake had still not got in touch. I didn't want to try calling him in case the line was being monitored by Purse, nor risk calling home for the same reason. I spent a lot of time just gazing at the street below. In the early mornings, the African workers waited to be picked up by the builders' trucks; then there was a long period of quiet until the siesta hour, when the girls began their shifts. Standing outside the old station, as if waiting for the ghosts of buses that would never come, they strutted and signalled for their punters, who passed in cars. One moment a girl would be there, and when I looked again she would be gone. Occasionally police cruisers drove by, paying no attention to anything that was happening.

A week passed this way, and I had begun to feel the danger was ebbing when I got a voice message from Bosano. There had been no more communications from Purse, and unsurprisingly he sounded relieved by this, but he had some rather strange news. He had heard that Elisabeth Dermot had been sighted several times in the past month, looking perfectly well and unharmed. My first reaction was to think there must be some mistake: I'd been asking everyone to look out for her, and had heard nothing of her for over a year. She was one of my oldest associates, and it seemed inconceivable that she wouldn't have contacted me to explain her absence or at least let me know she was all right. After such a long period without news, I had come to assume the worst.

When I left a return message for Bosano, asking for all the information he had, he came back saying it would be best if we met in person, and suggested the same *chiringuito* near Banus. Agreeing to this, but not taking any chances, I got there a couple of hours early and handed a note for Bosano to the barman, naming another location on the main strip in the port. It was much busier, so that if Bosano was being followed, or had been got to, it would have been riskier for Purse to try anything there. Unlike the single lane to the beach bar, it could be reached by many routes, and most were equally busy and public; in the back of my mind was the possibility that the Elisabeth story might be a bait to lure me out.

The bar was like an island amid the flow of tourists staring at the yachts, but when I ventured in at the agreed time, it turned out to be virtually empty inside. The front was filled with plastic jungle foliage and outsize, clip-on tropical parrots. The bar area was illuminated by a violet light that washed out the faces of the two sleepy-looking barmen and gave everything the hectic glow of radioactive material in cartoons.

I could make out Bosano already sitting at a corner table, facing the door. He was wearing a pair of Lennon specs and a worn corduroy jacket with leather patches on the arms. His baseball cap was pulled down low over his fat bullet head and the collar of his jacket was turned up, as if he were sitting out on a windy platform. It was not his usual get-up – more like the sort of thing worn by someone who wants to look cosy and trustworthy but isn't, almost a disguise. I wondered what he was playing at.

He rose immediately he saw me, making a lot of pulling out the table and plumping up the cushions before he would let me sit down. There were two dead cocktail glasses already on his side of the table, and close up under the light, his face had the glassy sweat of someone who had been drinking hard all day. Almost immediately he launched into one of his tedious urban myth stories, but the music was so loud and his voice so slurred that I only caught the general drift of it. It seemed to pivot on an idea I had heard somewhere before: that during the Spanish Civil War some of the Andalucian hill villages had for years become cut off from the outside world, and one of the most isolated of these had developed a taste for human flesh. Then, years later, young female holidaymakers had begun disappearing from the clubs in the Marbella area, their picked skeletons turning up on construction sites in the hills. I didn't hear the ending, nor was I interested, and I gestured to the sleepy-looking barman to turn down the music.

'Tell me about Elisabeth,' I said.

Bosano's glance drifted vaguely towards the tinted windows over the booth.

'This friend of mine knows her,' he said. He spoke quickly, almost impatiently, as if he half-expected me to know his lines already, like an actor at the end of a long run. 'He saw her at a club, and he mentioned it to me. So I guess she's alive.' He gave a short laugh.

'At a club? Are you sure? Who is this guy? Where did he see her?' Impatience was getting the better of me. I wanted it to be true, but something about this felt off.

Bosano fidgeted. 'In Campana – I don't think he said which club. And then he saw her again a week after, in La Linea de la Frontera.'

'What, he talked to her? Did they have a conversation? Why the hell would she be there?' La Linea de la Frontera was in the Campo de Gibraltar. Like the Campana district, it was one of the lowest *barrios* in the area, notable for street dealers and shooting galleries. These were no-go areas even for the police, places where one took one's life in one's hands just wandering around – definitely not the sort of places someone like Elisabeth would risk going alone, unless she had had a pressing reason. None of it added up, and Bosano seemed lost for a reply.

'What about Purse and Salomon? Any suggestion they're part of this?'

'I don't know,' was all Bosano could muster in response. He seemed uncomfortable with my incredulous reaction, and eager to get away. I pressed him a little further, but he really seemed to know nothing else, and I sat back, not bothering to hide my frustration. Apart from anything else, it was difficult to see why such paltry details couldn't have been given over the phone.

Bosano noticed me watching him and quickly looked down again, as if realizing he had already said enough. Lurching abruptly to his feet, he began patting down his pockets like a mime artist performing 'man who's left his wallet at home'. I let him suffer for a minute before raising my hand to call for the tab, then watched as he stumbled out through the violet light into the slow drift of couples along the front. Clearly he wasn't going to be a great deal of help in following up these supposed sightings; but following them up was now my priority. If Elisabeth really was safe and well, it was incredible news. If not, what reason could anyone have for inventing such a story? I intended to find out.

22

The honeycomb of apartment buildings in La Campana, where Bosano said Elisabeth had last been seen, had been built in the late sixties, about a kilometre inland from Banus on the outskirts of San Pedro de Alcántara. It mimicked the style of traditional Andalucian hill villages, but as with so many buildings in the area, the construction quality had been poor. Now large parts had fallen into disrepair, and were barely distinguishable from the ancient villages on which they had been modelled. I found the entrances to the squats and tenements at the heart of the district blocked by concrete slabs from nearby building works: no doubt they had been left there to discourage police vehicles from entering, although it was well-known that the local cops already did everything they could to avoid the area. I approached slowly, with the car doors locked and the windows closed. In a narrow isthmus between two of the slabs, an unofficial tollgate was being operated by local youths. I was reluctant to risk stopping and entering on foot, so I let them relieve me of a couple of thousand pesetas to take the car in. It looked like more trouble than it was worth to ask directions from any of the forlorn figures I passed, so I just kept circling through the maze of lanes until I found the club Bosano had finally named when I'd followed up our conversation by phone.

Other than the small flamingo-pink neon sign, the place looked no different on the outside from the other holes in the wall with bars and steel plates over them. It stood about twenty metres back from the road, the drive-way concealed by bushy jacarandas not cut back in the manner of most Spanish gardens. The rusting gates were tied together with twine and the intercom in the gatepost was dead. No doormen or other staff were visible around the covered portico, and I edged through the gates and let myself in.

Coming through the thick curtains, it took a few moments for my eyes to adjust to the dimness. A clutter of decorative objects – gilt mirrors, carved bed-heads, old church fittings – were stacked high against the walls, and further down a bar had been improvised from driftwood. To the far side of this was a small stage on which a couple of North African girls in thigh-high boots danced to Arabic music, in a dim imitation of some old Donna Summer routine; the girls' movements were sluggish, out of rhythm, as if they were swimming against some strong, slow-moving current. The only audience were other small groups of girls around low tables, without drinks in front of them, but none looked anything like Elisabeth. Most had the appearance of trafficked country girls from Eastern Europe, their pale skin and poorly dyed bobs reminding me of the girls outside the old bus station who waited on buses that would never come.

The nearest group appeared to be local women, too old now to be working the Golden Mile, their charms curdled by years in smoky clubs. I approached them cautiously. I was anticipating hostility when it became clear I was not a customer, but they looked at me impassively as I showed them the only pictures I'd been able to find of Elisabeth. They were from the seventies, but she was recognizably the same woman: her face with the same scrubbed look, no make-up, her straight hair with the same middle parting. But the women shook their heads without even checking the pictures. The same happened when I passed them to the Eastern European girls: they all looked back at me as if I was divided from them by some thick, unassailable partition. None were going to stick their necks out and risk trouble. Two men in bomber jackets had appeared and were now standing over me at the table, and a third in a leather coat was coming through the shadows behind them. I thought that maybe these were Salomon's henchmen, but their only interest was to get me to buy overpriced drinks from the bar. So I did, after which they clapped me on the back as if I was a good sport.

When I got outside again, my car was a mess: the mirrors, exhaust and catalytic convertor had all been ripped off, presumably to sell for scrap. I should have realized that this was going to happen here. I left the rest of my enquiries about Elisabeth for the following day and returned to Torremolinos, where I left the car at a garage on the outskirts and took a taxi back to the Portillo. Still confident that no one would track me down in such a place, I went straight up without checking with the *portero* if anyone had been round asking questions.

The flat looked the same as when I had left it, and I rolled a joint and went out on the terrace to wind down. But when I called Bosano to tell him I had got nowhere, he sounded graver than usual and had some disturbing news. He had heard from a police contact that a body that might have been Elisabeth's had been found in La Linea de la Frontera – in an area where bodies from local gang wars were often dumped. The body had already been there for some weeks, maybe even longer.

It was a crushing blow. I had suspected Elisabeth's fate had not been a good one, but the thought of her body lying in such a place like some piece of trash was almost too much to bear. And if it was true, what on earth had been happening in my old friend's life for the past year? I put the phone down mid-sentence, and could not go on with the conversation. Immediately I took all the sleepers I had, the remains of my stock from Valletta. Though there was still enough uncertainty in the situation to keep some hope alive, I felt low as hell, as low as I've ever felt. I wanted to call home but, knowing the risks of making even a single call and revealing my location to Purse, held back.

I rose early the next day, picked up the car and drove straight to La Linea de la Frontera along the new road, avoiding the smaller resorts along the way. I was early for my appointment at the police station with Bosano's contact. The new police building was well signed, no more than minutes away from the border, a modern construction with walls topped with wire, a reception area that still smelt of paint. The girl there told me it would be safer if I left the car in the station, as the area had a worse reputation even than La Campana. I had no intention of exposing my car or my person to any more risks than were necessary, so was relieved when Bosano's officer, an Inspector Pérez, ushered me down to his own car. He was the man who was going to help me find out whether the body that they had discovered was indeed Elisabeth's. But first he was going to take me to the spot where they had found the corpse.

Pérez was in his early thirties, probably still living at home with his parents, like most Spaniards of his age. Once we were in the car, he smiled tensely as if he were doing something against his better judgement, and didn't say much at first. His few remarks to me on the phone had suggested he was one of the new breed of university-educated Spanish policemen, his English surprisingly fluent, with a slight northern inflection. At first he seemed more interested in showing off his English to me than saying much that was useful. I imagined that he'd had regular opportunities to practise on the small army of foreign junkies drawn to his area by the cheap smack, which leaked off the shipments over the straits. To most expats, La Linea de la Frontera was just an obstacle on their way to stock up at Safeways and the other supermarkets in Gibraltar: such was its reputation for street crime and general lawlessness that on reaching the outskirts they would lock the car doors and accelerate hard down its dusty seafront boulevards, never stopping at the *chiringuitos* and bars set up along the roadside to lure passing trade.

Though the place was looking a little more prosperous than I remembered, this was most likely just a sign of local gang money finding its way into the light. At the eastern approach to the seafront were a new sun-bleached car dealership and two new furniture superstores covered in hoardings and scaffolding. It all smelt of black money. The air freshened for a minute as the road ran parallel to the sea, and ahead through the mist the east face of the Rock rose sheer over the bay, reminiscent in its shape and colouring of a giant loaf of bread gone stale and hard in the sun. Overlooking the grey waters there were two brand-new hotels, probably also gang laundry vehicles, their car parks both empty. This was not an area people tended to stop overnight. Along the front were other recently opened businesses: amusement arcades, a funfair, all empty also. This was an emptiness that seemed more than seasonal, and through the windows of the roadside bars, where the expats never stopped, were glimpses of set tables standing in empty dining rooms. Below on the beach, linen was hanging out on drying poles over the sand, flapping in the breeze over the bay like flags of surrender.

Here Pérez turned inland, into narrow streets between rows of low-rise tenements. The Rock abruptly disappeared from view, so that it was difficult to get one's bearings. Looking at the street map taped to the console, I saw we must have begun moving westwards, through the closely knit alleys which lay between the bay and the newer parts of the town to the south. The buildings were the same type of squat, single-storey concrete-fronted houses that lined the front, but most of the shops between them had been boarded up. In the crossroads between the alleys, the only stores were windowless liquor stands, their hatches covered with metal and wire mesh; the few figures outside them were wearing baseball caps pulled low, and they all turned away and hid their faces when they saw the police car approaching. It was difficult to imagine what Elisabeth could have been doing in such a place, and I could only think she had been brought here against her will.

The way continued inwards between more derelict and burnt-out buildings, and we saw no one in the dusty clearings between them. Was this really where Elisabeth had ended her days? A series of dog-legged alleys came out onto an expanse of waste ground before the streets petered out altogether. The buildings that had once stood there had all been levelled, and I guessed we had now reached the edges of the closed-off district. 'A lot of bodies wash up here,' Pérez said matter-of-factly. Ahead was a concrete wall about seven metres high, covered in tag graffiti and stretching about four blocks; the structure circled back on itself to enclose an oval about half a kilometre square, and was high enough to hide whatever eyesores were within from the cluster of newer blocks back towards the sea.

The abruptness with which the wall cut through the desolate space reminded me of photographs of the perimeter wall of the Warsaw ghetto, and of the way sections of the Berlin wall had cut through that divided city. Under the wall, a deep trench had been dug that ran along its length for as far as we could see; halfway along, planks had been laid to allow access to a single narrow gap in the wall's smooth face. Pérez explained that originally the municipality had built the wall to keep people away from the dangerous ruins and tunnels inside, but the area had become infested with junkies and drug gangs. Now there was only the one way in and out; at night, the police never entered except in large deployments. Inside they had no control over what happened. He said all this in the tone of a tour guide who had spoken variations of the same words before to audiences he would never have to see again.

He was still smiling his same thin smile, and as we moved away from the stalls with their hatches covered in wire, he gestured back at them and began telling me an anecdote. When he had first worked in the district he had once stopped at one of the stalls to buy some juice from the old couple inside, and had noticed a photograph of the same pair when younger in a fine, airy shop with bottle-green tiles on the walls and piles of fresh fruit outside. He had wondered what sort of madmen would leave a fine shop like that, and go into business amid all the dereliction – but then, as he left, he'd noticed that the tiles behind the shack had once been bottle-green and the charred walls, where the hatch stood, had once been a large shop open to the street. He discovered that when the area had gone down the couple had been unable to sell up, and over the years their business had slowly adapted to the demands of their new environment. Later, both their daughters had become addicts and died, but the couple had too many debts to move, and so had no choice but to stay on and work their stall.

As we walked along, Pérez was indicating that I should keep a couple of steps behind him. I followed him along the trench opposite the gap. Despite what he had just said about the lack of police control over the area, he showed no hesitation as he advanced over the rubble, and I wondered if he hadn't exaggerated the dangers slightly.

He crossed the planks in three easy strides and waited for me at the far end. Even if I fell into the trench, the worst that could happen would be sprained ankles and bruised dignity, but it still took an effort of will to make the few steps across. I kept my eyes on the featureless wall ahead. Once through the gap, we made our way up another narrow alley where the air was fetid and houses were so close that their roofs touched in places, the daylight falling across the dirt floor in thin, dull strips. Pérez kept looking back over his shoulder, though the alley around us was silent. After about a minute of advancing in this way, he signalled that we should turn right into a passageway where stone steps led down the side of a house.

There was no key, nor any keyhole to be seen. Admittance could only be gained by throwing one's weight against it. Pérez produced heavy gardening gloves, the type used to move embers from a fire, and put them on.

'Keep your hands in your pockets, okay? All the time. Otherwise you could catch a needle.'

He fished a small torch out of his pocket, and I followed him into the dark. The walls of the tunnel were beaded with moisture and smelt of rotten fish, the torch's beam bouncing over the vaulting above our heads. Further up, I knew, the rock was almost hollow with caves and tunnels. Over the centuries the natural formations had been extended, first by the Moors and later by the British, into an interlocking network. A whole city had been built underground, where the power plants and the water depots for the town were now situated; but down this far, on the level of the plain, most of the tunnels were built only in the last two centuries to store the contraband brought in by boat from across the straits. Unlike the tunnels up in the rock, this lower system had never been mapped, and by closing off this section of the town, where the entrances were located, the municipality had presumably hoped to limit access to it. In such a place, it was lucky to have found a body at all. Bodies could lie underground for months until they were unrecognizable; sometimes they were quietly buried by the inhabitants, and the person just disappeared forever.

Every few moments Pérez kept stopping and looking about, as if half-expecting to spot something ghastly in the water. He seemed uncertain of the way, and was calling ahead in Spanish phrases I did not understand, his tone light and tentative, as if he were trying out some new witticism for the first time on strangers. There was no response, nor any echoes from within. As we went on, the ceilings became lower and the floor rougher and more waterlogged. I felt the water rising over the tops of my shoes, and several times I almost lost my footing. I could sense the tunnel was reaching back under the houses by the beach, and at one point I could hear the tidal swell lapping against a hollow somewhere nearby. Even for those who knew the tunnels, I felt it must have seemed a remote and rarely visited place.

I knew that I could have told Pérez I had seen enough, and within minutes he would have conveyed us back into the light, but I had to see the place for myself. My sense of time was already distorted from being underground: I was not sure how long we had been walking when he suddenly stopped and shone his torch onto the ground. There was no outline in white, as I had seen in films of crime scenes, to mark where the body had lain. Nothing to distinguish the place, apart from some candle stubs and two damp foam cushions. I wondered if this was really it; could he be just guessing, choosing a spot that looked likely to save himself more trouble?

He kept moving the torch in an arc. From behind the wall, I could hear a light yet persistent pattering in the shallow water, but I supposed the torch and our voices were keeping whatever was there from coming out onto the floor. No other sounds entered the low chamber, and I could no longer hear the sea. Under the wall, from where the pattering rose like a short-wave frequency, sat a plastic torch and fold-up ladder, both bearing the crest of the town hall, left behind by the municipal workers who had discovered the body. I knew it would look bad if I hurried away from the place too quickly, but I had to take deep breaths so as to fight the urge to leave at once. In truth, there was no more to see there than what had been apparent at first glance.

On the journey back, Pérez hardly spoke to me at all. With each new query from me, his manner only seemed to become more reserved. I expected him to show me some photographs and request my assistance in the identification of the body, but he did not do this. Perhaps he felt I was already too shaken. To start with, he just said that some papers found on the body relating to a flat Elisabeth had owned through a holding company in Palma de Mallorca had led to the initial identification being made. That, and the fact that she had apparently been missing for a year. The identification would not be confirmed formally until dental records had arrived from England. In the meantime her body had been removed and was being kept in the morgue at the hospital in Algeciras, a larger town five kilometres up the coast. Pérez stressed again that we were fortunate the body had been found at all, as in a few months the whole area was to be bulldozed to make way for a regeneration project.

Until the dental records surfaced, I supposed there was still some hope, but I did not cling to it. I hated the open-ended uncertainty in the situation. In the past, I had always prepared myself for moments like this by anticipating the worst outcome; that way, one was never disappointed. Somehow, this strategy only seemed to be making the situation worse. I felt I needed a drink.

After Pérez dropped me off at the police station, I drove around for a while in a daze. I followed the avenue down from the police station and came again to the empty beach cafes and the small houses that looked as if they had once been fishermen's cottages. Behind them stood the stands with metal shutters. Buying a quarter litre of whisky from the nearest, I sat in the car for an hour or so, just gazing out into space. It was difficult to picture what was going to happen next.

I remember an elderly woman in a widow's black housecoat, emptying a bucket of suds onto the pavement, waiting for the water to spread to its furthest extent, then setting about the pavement with a stiff-bristled brush. Further along, two old men stood talking as two mongrels circled each other between their legs. Beneath them, by an upturned boat, in the lee of a kiosk boarded up until the summer, an adolescent boy sat mending a fishing net. The beach was separated from the pavement by a line of concrete blocks that ran as far as it was possible to see on either side. I got out and stood looking out at the sea, inhaling the scents of the upturned boats mixed with the odour of the rotting sardine scraps from down on the dunes.

Between the hunt for Bowen's stash, the Zurich deal,

getting mixed up with the Brink's-Mat bullion and Elisabeth disappearing, I was struggling to keep track of what was going on anymore. Behind me, I could hear the crackle of discarded packets and sweet wrappers being brushed along the pavement by the wind. From the concrete blocks, I walked across to the row of small cafes converted from the cottages' former front parlours. I sat at one of the tables, and waited as another old woman took my order. Being near the sea out of season always made me think of the drenched shores of Wales, and the dark grit down on the beach seemed to merge into the broad rain-sodden sands of my childhood.

It had been on mornings like this that we walked to Sket with picnic baskets and beach umbrellas. The routine when we got there had always been the same: with the westerlies blowing sand over the food, we got down to lunch immediately, the adults joking that the gritty substance on their hard-boiled eggs was more sand than salt. Afterwards, we held competitions to see who could stay in the water the longest. However warm the day, the sea had always been icy, and a minute's stint of shivering and hopping from one foot to the other had usually been sufficient for victory.

When the wind and sand had finally defeated us, we faced the trek back to the ridge. The picnic baskets should have been lighter, yet had always seemed heavier, and on reaching the top, as a reward for making the ascent without complaint, we had been bought our '99s from the van parked on the crumbled strip of tarmac. We had competed to lick the ice cream away as slowly as possible around the chocolate, each trying to hold out for longer than the other before biting into the flake itself. Then on the way home there had always been the stop for tea at Jenny Hopkins' cafe and teashop situated right in the middle of Kenfig Hill. The food was always the same: fairy cakes topped with icing and a quarter of a glacé cherry, and buttered scones served with pots of clotted cream and raspberry jam. The crockery was a mismatched assortment of milky glassware, with cups and saucers so thick we struggled to drink from them.

The old woman was looking over from the counter to see if I was finished. Through the door behind her, covered with plastic beads, came the pleasant aroma of baking bread, mingling with the scents of the dunes below. Down on the beach, some couples were strolling now with dogs along the edges of the wash. On the promenade, the two old men had not moved far between the palms. By the upturned boat, under the boarded-up kiosk, the boy still sat mending his net, looking up at the empty avenue.

23

There was no doubt in my mind at this stage: I badly needed a break from everything, a change of scene. If nothing else, taking a step back from the tangle of anxieties about Purse, Bowen, Elisabeth, and my own apparently dwindling career and life prospects, seemed the best strategy of seeing my way forward out of the mess.

Using Madrid Barajas airport rather than any of the smaller local ones like Malaga or Seville (which I suspected Purse might still be monitoring), I flew back to London. It was now late spring of 1999, and I intended to go on to the Far East for a few weeks on the invitation of an old friend from Oxford, Daniel Topolski, who had some rather delicate business in Manila to deal with.

Topolski had been in my year at university, where we had been firm friends. He had been part of the victorious teams in several Oxford–Cambridge boat races and had become coach for the Oxford team, winning twelve out of fifteen successive encounters with Cambridge. It was difficult, on the face of it, to imagine a person less connected to what had been going on in my life recently, and I should have felt safe in his company – but I was a little surprised to hear from him out of the blue at such a moment.

At the back of my mind was a suspicion that this might be another, more circuitous overture from Purse. I vaguely remembered that Topolski's father, an official World War Two war artist who had also worked for the Queen, had exhibited at one of the galleries Purse owned in London. It was a tenuous connection, but it was enough to put me on my guard. Topolski told me initially only that the matter concerned Colin Moynihan, former Minister for Sport in Thatcher's government. I knew that Colin was the half-brother of the late Lord Tony Moynihan, the DEA informer in the case against me. Alarm bells began to sound, but as Topolski was an old friend, I was willing to hear him out.

Topolski emphasized that Colin Moynihan was a good friend of his, and was now interested in investigating the circumstances of his half-brother's death. He was willing to pay my travel expenses if I would accompany Topolski to interview Joe Smith, a well-known Australian mari-juana smuggler and member of the Double Bay mob. It was common knowledge that Tony Moynihan had informed on Smith to the Australian embassy in Manila; Smith therefore had a motive for seeing Moynihan dead. Now Colin wanted us to travel to Manila to interview those who had been close to Tony – and it was implied that this was an opportunity for me to clear my own name, as I myself had been in the frame as responsible for Moynihan's death seven years earlier.

Normally such a mission would not have appealed to me. In fact, I would have avoided anything to do with Moynihan like the plague; but now, with so many unanswered questions about Bowen and Purse, and Elisabeth's body still not having been positively identified, I felt I needed to see whether Topolski was playing with a straight bat or not, and whether there was a connection on this front I had not anticipated, which would illuminate everything else. Topolski then introduced me to Colin, who explained he intended to archive any information we obtained in Manila for his personal use only, and had no intention of publishing it. Colin had spent the last five years successfully proving his claim to his title, which had been dormant after Tony's sudden death. He had proved this on the grounds that one of Tony's sons was not in fact his, and the other was the offspring of a bigamous marriage; he said his interest now was simply finding out how Tony had died, for his own personal satisfaction. During these proceedings I brought up Purse and Bowen several times with both Topolski and Colin Moynihan, but neither seemed to have any direct connection with either figure. On the surface, at least, it appeared that the Moynihan trip was totally unconnected to the Bowen matter.

On the way in from the airport in Manila we passed

the old MacArthur Hotel, now renamed, which Tony Moynihan had owned and tried to get me to invest in. It brought back mixed memories. As an inducement to my investing, Tony had offered to make my travel agency the sole representative in London for Philippines Airlines. He had named a suite in the hotel after me. He had also offered to buy land on an island north of the mainland called Fuga to facilitate the growing of cannabis – and it was this plan which had proved so fatal when he had discussed it with me while wearing a DEA wire.

At first sight it appeared Manila had been cleaned up significantly since my last visit, and the old massage parlour district, Del Pilar, seemed to have vanished altogether. However, as we began moving about the next day by the local small bus called a jeepney, it became apparent that this side of the city had simply shifted location further west. We called on the former consul, Brian Lane, for information about Moynihan's death. Lane assumed I had come to Manila for the purposes of blackening Moynihan's name as Moynihan had informed on me, and he insisted that Moynihan had only worn a wire under heavy pressure from the DEA agents heading the team investigating me. Whether Lane really knew much or not about Moynihan's death, I am not certain, but he appeared not to.

Next we called on Moynihan's fifth and last wife, Jinna, who still lived in Moynihan's old house, formerly the Peruvian embassy; I had visited him there many times and discussed our growing plans in the northern islands. We were received hospitably and shown Moynihan's grave. Over the next few days we called on his fourth wife, Editha, and did the rounds of the expat bars and the small circle Moynihan had associated with in his final months. It was at this point that Spencer Purse's name began to crop up in conversation.

The first time his name was mentioned was as a potential investor in the MacArthur Hotel. Then it was floated that he had been operating a laboratory on one of the northern islands. Given both my previous life, and the nature of the business I now found myself in, it seemed inevitable that wherever I turned now Bowen or Purse was there waiting for me in some form or other. But further enquiries showed that Purse's presence in Manila had post-dated Moynihan's death and had been brief, and I wondered if this was just an unfortunate coincidence. Even more fortuitously, it seemed that he had not been seen since.

A couple more days of asking questions led us to an establishment called the Irish Grill, where Moynihan had met his end. After interviewing the owner, a certain Billy Kelly, I was satisfied there had in fact been no foul play and Moynihan had simply died of a heart attack after eating a heavy Irish stew. This story had clearly become something of a set piece for Kelly, though it did not necessarily reflect well on his cuisine. He even accompanied it with some theatrics; but after having reached my own conclusions, I struggled to engage with the conversation any further.

Topolski had been excellent company throughout the trip, but I was preoccupied by the mess I had left behind. Previously, when I had spent so much time of my life on the run, or moving quickly from one deal to the next, it had been possible – indeed, necessary – to live completely in the moment. True, I had been stoned much of that time, unlike now; but the years had caught up with me, even if prison life itself had left little mark. What I really wanted was the one thing that I could not have, but had promised myself – a quiet life with my family. My mind kept focusing, involuntarily, on what had happened over the last few months, as if somehow going over it repeatedly would make more sense of events; but it didn't.

If I had hoped things would be calmer on my return to the chalet near Estepona, I was to be disappointed. I'd been back for less than a day when Bosano called to say that the Elisabeth Dermot matter was no further forward. As dental records had not yet been recovered from England, no positive identification of the body could yet be made. On other matters, there was still no sign of Drake, who I had not spoken to for months, even though the plan had been to get together to ship the remaining stash from Zurich. Purse and Salomon had been phoning Bosano four or five times every day, wanting to know whether I had called in yet.

Taking the bull by the horns, I called Salomon, getting through to him straight away on the last number he had phoned me from. I put to him in the strongest terms that he and Purse were wasting their time on me. I did my best to make clear that if Drake had access to Bowen's gear, he certainly had not told me anything about this. I explained that I had been misdirected into thinking it had come from India, and that I had no idea of the location of either Drake, or the missing gear.

Although I was direct and entirely truthful, Salomon sounded sceptical. A few minutes later he called back and said that the best way forward was for me to explain the situation to Purse in person. He gave me the address of a villa in Madroñal, and said Purse would be waiting for me there that evening.

It should not have surprised me that Purse was down on the coast, as the Bowen matter was obviously so important to him. Still, the revelation that he was so near – no more than twenty minutes' drive from where I sat – gave me a jolt. I had misgivings about going to see him alone, but by making the meet at a pre-arranged place and time, Salomon was probably signalling that I had safe passage. Experienced criminals rarely make prior arrangements with a person if they intend to abduct or kill them, and Salomon was well aware that I could have informed third parties of who I was meeting. Still, as nothing had been said explicitly, I knew that I needed to cover myself. I called Bosano and Jacobs, who was in London, to let them know where I was going, and what to do if I had not made contact by the evening.

An hour before the appointed time, I made my way to Madroñal up through the hills from San Pedro de Alcántara. The upper parts appeared almost dark, as most of the properties there were only occupied for a few weeks in the summer. That Purse should have had a villa there was rather predictable, as the area contained some of the largest properties on the coast. Originally just barren scrub, belonging to a local landowner called Don Jaime Parlade, gradually it had been parcelled off. Electricity and water had been brought in from the town below, and several German industrialists had bought properties there, along with some more established British criminals. Most of the land faced east towards the Concha mountain and Marbella town, the other side enjoying the preferable sunset views over the Straits of Gibraltar and the Atlas mountains. The villas up on those higher slopes rarely sold for under ten million pounds.

The address I was looking for was in this most desirable section, overlooking the village of Benahavis and with views of the straits. My route took me past the ritzy car showrooms opposite Banus port, and past the Centro Plaza hotel, where one wing was lit up for a convention.

On the seaboard side, the lights of Banus were visible as a glow through the umbrella pines. Occasional strips of overpriced supermercados and farmacias alternated with the gates of villas under clusters of mature palms, their high walls cutting off the remaining views down to the coast. The road circled up between the hills, passing the shells of blocks left over from the last property crash of the late eighties. Through gaps in the trees could be glimpsed the larger, vague shapes of the grander villas on the ridges above.

Eventually a high stone wall came into view ahead, topped with spirals of barbed wire and running on to a gate set under a whitewashed arch. From this distance, the house beyond it looked more like a child's drawing of a mansion than the real thing – it was enormous. The windows at the front were shuttered against the winds and the plants around the porch covered in plastic sheeting, which rippled and ballooned in the gusts. A Filipino in uniform met me at the door and ushered me over the wide expanse of the hall, up a double staircase, embassy-like in its grandeur, and through a formal sitting room and several offices; along the walls were lines of *kists* supporting a series of gilded Egyptian death masks and statues of Anubis, the jackal-headed god. Beyond them lay a home cinema room and an office lined with smoked-glass mirrors.

Purse was waiting for me in the office, looking as tense as he had in Norfolk. When I declined his offer of a chair, he tried not to look offended, and insisted I join him for dinner. I was not in the mood for politeness. I accused him of going through my room at the Groucho and leaving the dog. He said nothing. There was a brief, awkward, silent stand-off between us; then a laid table was brought in, and a man who must have been Purse's personal chef came in and announced in a thick French accent what we were about to be served.

Once we were seated, Purse seemed to relax a little.

'Last time we met, I wasn't completely straight with you,' he began. 'Everything relating to Bowen was coming to me from Juan Royal. But I can assure you, Howard –' he gave me an intense look – 'I intend to be straight with you now.'

I felt he expected me to understand some hidden significance in these words, but I wasn't sure I did. All I knew was what had been implied by our previous talk: that Purse needed Royal if he was going to get into the lucrative American market, and to achieve that end he would probably do anything Royal wanted. In this situation, Royal's reasons for wanting things done were largely irrelevant to Purse – only that they had to be done.

Purse kept circling back to the same point: Royal had told him Bowen's gear had fallen into the wrong hands, and Royal wanted the gear destroyed at all costs before it reached the market. I waited for an explanation. Purse stressed that, according to Royal, failure to do this would be catastrophic for the ecstasy market. But the more I thought about this, the less sense it made. However large the Bowen consignment was – and it was certainly one of the biggest of all time – it could only affect the market briefly. It was just a single event, not a new in-flow: even if the quality had been adulterated, the pressure on prices would only be temporary. If Drake was calling the shots, then the likelihood was that the gear would go into the European market, where Royal had only a patchy presence. It was difficult to see what Royal was so concerned about, and his request that the gear be destroyed seemed extreme and nonsensical.

I suspected Purse did not fully understand that aspect either: his wide-eyed expression suggested he shared my bewilderment. But it was clear he didn't care what Royal's reason was: he simply wanted the job done, and was focusing on the reward.

'I know you're a man of your word,' he told me. 'I want you to swear that you'll contact me if Drake comes back onto your radar, and I want your help in making a connection with him – or with the gear. If you can do that for me, there's something in it for you, of course.' He named a frankly ridiculous sum of money, half a million sterling, and more at a later date if I kept playing ball.

I allowed myself to imagine for a moment that I might agree to this plan. I couldn't deny it was tempting; and, as it seemed Drake had misled me, it might have been possible to justify it to myself. Deep down, though, I knew I couldn't betray Drake; it simply wasn't the way I worked, and no amount of money would make it sit well with my conscience.

I took a deep breath, and looked Purse in the eye. 'I appreciate the offer,' I said truthfully. 'But I can't promise that. I will give you my word, though, that I will no longer actively look for the rest of Bowen's gear. That's as far as I can go with this.'

Purse's expression acknowledged polite disappointment, but he didn't look particularly surprised. The discussion went back and forth a little longer, but contrary to my expectation, he didn't apply pressure. By the end of the meal, I had the sense he'd accepted what I'd said. I left the villa that night feeling as if some, if not quite all, of the weight had been lifted from my shoulders.

24

Despite what I had told Purse, as the summer of '99 approached I did make some more discreet enquiries about Drake's whereabouts. Mutual acquaintances suggested he was hiding from Purse, and from the world in general. He hadn't been seen in London, nor in Madrid, and no one had any idea where he was.

The few enquiries I continued to make about Bowen – again, more discreetly than before – got nowhere either. He seemed to have moved largely unnoticed through the world and left few traces of his activities, and attempts to find out if he had used a property in the country as a lab had brought no results. Not for the first time, I felt I had reached a dead end and would never find the truth. From time to time, I even found myself doubting whether there had ever been a stash at all; perhaps it was just a myth that people wanted to believe in. Deep down, though, I knew Purse was not someone who would waste time on phantoms; and what he had said about Royal suggested a real enough, if still unexplained, fear.

My diary for the rest of 1999 was now filling up again with a series of new dates for the show based on my autobiography, and several guest DJ slots at clubs in Manchester, Norwich and London. The owners of the Manumission rave franchise, Mike McKay and Claire Davies, had asked me to be writer-in-residence at their mega-club in Ibiza for three weeks later in the year. I had agreed to do this, as it sounded like good fun, decent money and a way to keep me occupied. The rave was known to be the world's biggest regular party, hosting 10,000 clubbers and turning over at least a million pounds' worth of ticket sales and alcohol a night. There were at least another million pounds' worth of MDMA sales every night, too. It seemed too good an opportunity to miss.

For the first time in many months, I had begun to slip back into using ecstasy on an almost daily basis. I was friendly with the Welsh band Super Furry Animals, who had used my picture on one of their album covers, and was regularly invited to parties given by other bands on their Creation label. Although the label was now half-owned by Sony, it was still run by Alan McGee, who had been courted by Labour during the election year to run their media campaign. McGee, once an ecstasy head, had cleaned up his act, but the scene around him was still fuelled by the drug, and it was easy to score at such events. I also still had some samples of the pure MDMA from the first half of the Zurich scam at hand, which it was tempting to dip into. I was still putting off the second half, owing to the risks involved – and whenever Jacobs or anyone representing Drake called to expedite matters, I fobbed them off – but as funds began running low, I wasn't averse to knocking out small amounts of powder to generate cash flow.

Returning to Malaga via Barajas airport in Madrid, I had taken my usual small amount of cannabis wrapped in wax, along with a float of about twenty grams of the powder for my own personal use. The cannabis was simply for smoking in the toilets if the flight was delayed; these quantities were more or less compatible with personal use, and I was not anticipating any problems. I had not reckoned, however, on the flight being full of a rowdy Ibiza crowd taking an onward connection. In the front row, DJ Snoop and the Vibrating Eggs were having a party; Mike McKay and Claire Davies were also on board, getting intimate in full view, and there were more DJs in the back. When the No Smoking sign went off, the heady aroma of Nepalese was filling the cabin. On arrival at Barajas, predictably enough, Customs were all over us, and most passengers were ushered into cubicles for strip searches. Fortunately, as an old hand at the game, I still had a trick or two up my sleeve, and I followed my usual practice of coming at the rear of the passenger column so that I could see what kind of measures were in place ahead. Unlike in Mallorca, the route in from the plane was all indoors, and security was tighter due to recent ETA activity. I had to abandon my wax parcel halfway, with no hope of being able to retrieve it at a later date.

At my request, the following day Jacobs posted me another small float of MDMA powder, which arrived safely. My usage continued, but in a more modest form. I had not been suffering from cell shock, or agoraphobia, for over twelve months, as I had formerly among the crowds in London, and no longer had any therapeutic need for the drug. I just took it now to pass the time and connect in a more immediate, unmediated way to my surroundings. Once he knew I had some quality gear in the house Bosano began dropping round again every few days, usually without giving much notice, because he was a hound for anything quality. When I passed him the wrap, expecting him to take out a line, he put his nose right in and began snorting. Nothing good was going to come of this; and sure enough, without asking my permission, Bosano gave my address to a couple of his friends from Gibraltar, who he owed favours to. They came round late at night, obviously drunk, asking for gear, thinking I was some sort of neighbourhood dealer. When I refused them entry they sat outside in their car playing loud house music, and I had to phone Bosano to get them to go away. For obvious reasons, I told him to make sure this did not happen again.

Though his having given my address out was a liberty,

I had to tread carefully with Bosano due to his helpful role in finding out about Elisabeth Dermot, and so did not make too much of the incident. Bosano seemed contrite enough, apologizing profusely and assuring me it had all been a misunderstanding. The next day he returned for a further clearing of the air with one of the group, who he introduced as Gary Mascarenas, a business associate from Gibraltar. As it happened, I had met Gary several times before at Dreamers club in Banus, but neither he nor Bosano could remember this: it seemed they just wanted me to work with them on what they termed a 'shared ownership resort project'. This, I gathered, was simply a new term for a timeshare, the name having changed because the industry had such a poor reputation. Over the following days, Bosano was pushing the project hard and seemed unable to talk about anything else.

It was no secret that timeshare was still a popular investment vehicle for British criminals, as it was relatively risk-free and generated returns far in excess of what could be made from most legitimate business. I didn't want to alienate Bosano, so I didn't definitively rule out getting involved. A couple of days later he and Mascarenas drove me out to a strip ten kilometres east of Marbella, near the budget resort of Elviria, to explain the business model and talk through potential returns.

The first thing they stressed was that the hotels on which the business was based were stable assets that could always be sold on. According to Mascarenas, who was presenting himself as the senior partner in the scam, the rest of the business model could best be understood in terms of a rigged lottery: in a normal lottery, a punter worked out the odds against the number of tickets issued, but a bent lottery issued more tickets than the numbers suggested, so stacked the odds against the punter. This could be done by having several series of the same numbers, but prefixing them with letters, so each punter who bought the number ten would believe his was the only ticket of that number: there might in fact be ten of them, and only one valid in the draw. For the scheme to work effectively, the prizes in the bent lottery had to be so tempting that they would over-ride the natural caution of the investor.

Similarly, those who bought membership in a time-share resort were lured by the mirage of luxury the resort offered them. They were promised a certain amount of weeks per year free in the resort, but many more weeks were sold than the resort could accommodate. When they attempted to book their weeks, the buyers would then find the small print in their contracts, which allowed the resort to shift them to non-peak times of year, or charge them additional fees for their stay. To add insult to injury, the show-flats rarely bore any resemblance to the actual accommodation in which the buyers were housed, and the resorts were often deliberately isolated from their surroundings so that buyers were dependent on the over-priced facilities in the resort.

It was a lucrative but low-hitting scam, and I wanted no part in it. In any case, it turned out Bosano and Mascarenas didn't even own any shares in the business yet: they planned to spy on the practices of the resort and then have it busted by some officials from the town hall they had paid off, before coming in with their takeover bid. The whole thing felt like trouble, and badly thought out. I planned to go along with them only so far as was necessary to keep the peace, and then find some excuse to absent myself.

The day they picked me up, we drove straight over to a tourist cafe, where we sat at dusk on the Elviria seafront. Mascarenas assured me that their research showed this cafe to be one of those regularly targeted by the touts who lured holidaymakers up to the resort complex in nearby Calahonda for sales presentations. The place had certainly not been selected for its culinary appeal: the tortillas we had ordered from the photo-menu were made with frozen chips, and as I sipped my beer I could taste washing-up liquid on the glass. But it was not long before we began to notice a group of young women weaving their way between the tables, singling out the tourists from the other side of the road and moving in among them, handing out what appeared to be free draws in scratch card competitions. Most wore pin-badges or baseball-style jackets, with the name of the resort on the back. Bosano caught the eye of a mixed-race girl with her hair in cornrows, and she quickly homed in on us.

The scratch card the girl handed us had a winning row of three dolphins, and we were congratulated on having won a Sanyo mini-system: we could collect this if we accompanied her to the resort in Calahonda. We were shown round to a minibus parked in the alley behind, where about half a dozen elderly pensioner couples were already waiting, and a ten-minute trip took us to three identical barrack-like blocks.

Outside, several large billboards facing the main road indicated that the company was looking for new staff. On closer inspection these appeared weathered, as if they were a permanent feature of the place. All the blocks overlooked the same narrow beach of imported grey sand. The drive appeared recently tarmacked and on each side of it was a row of immature palms, still in their sacking sheaths. The place smelt as if it had all just been refurbished, the scents of new paint and adhesive coming through under the fragrance of cheap potpourri that flowed across the lobby. Through smoked-glass doors a central courtyard was visible, planted like the drive with new palmettos and low-maintenance shrubs; but despite the apparent size of the resort, we could see no sign of any other guests, and there was something of an empty stage set about the place.

In the lobby, a line of women in electric-blue suits and

heavy make-up received us with the practised smiles of
stewardesses on a long-haul flight. The prizes they handed
out were wrapped in many layers of opaque cellophane,
but before we could try to open them we were ushered
through to a show-flat on the ground floor, which conveniently had an access ramp for the elderly and those
in wheelchairs. On the side table were several jugs of a
strong-smelling punch. Our hostesses handed this out
with the impatient solicitude of shift carers dispensing
medication in an old people's home.

The rooms were a superficially impressive amalgam of
hi-tech fittings and pastel leather furnishings; the women
were immediately taken aside to be shown the eye-level
oven and other features in the kitchen, while the men were
invited to examine the satellite TV and Linn sound system
in the living room. When I slipped into the bathroom for
a quick smoke, the floor and ceiling were all covered in a
livid green stone into which had been sunk full-length mirrors with gold stud surrounds, and what looked like a fish
tank, but was revealed to be a plasma screen showing a
tropical reef. In the corner, a door led through to a steam
room with oak-effect panelling. By this stage I had managed to unwrap the gift and found it contained an ancient
Walkman, without its original packaging. It had scratches
on the casing, as though it had already spent a lot of time
in someone's pocket knocking against car keys or small
change.

The sauna in the bathroom was making me perspire, and though I wiped myself down with one of the display towels, I still came out looking sweaty and unkempt. I was now attracting some strange looks from the group, and Bosano and Mascarenas were giving me loaded glances; fortunately, the action was moving out onto the balcony. The flat had a view directly down to the thin grey strip of beach, and our guide kept pointing at this as if it were some kind of marvel. The reactions of the group suggested that they were indeed impressed by it.

Below, we could now see several women wearing the same blue suits as our guide and her colleagues who had received us in the lobby. Bosano explained that these women were known in the timeshare trade as 'sizzlers'. They were mostly recruited from hostess bars and casinos, and trained for a specific role in the industry: their brief was to prime the 'ups' – those brought 'up' from the cafes by the touts – before the 'closers' moved in. They were chosen for their looks and charm, and they aimed their pitches at the wives, as research had shown it was the wives who always made decisions about holiday accommodation. As Bosano put it, they were meant to be the type of women the men wanted to sleep with and the wives looked up to and wanted to be.

Another identical minibus was now pulling in, with several more elderly couples on board. Its driver, a blonde-haired girl who looked as if she'd only just left school, got out and ushered the couples in towards the lobby. Bosano explained that these 'timeshare touts' were known in the trade as OPCs – outside personal contacts – and the scratch cards they used were rigged: they were all winners. The OPCs got paid by the amount of ups they brought into the resort, and they only got paid for couples, never for singles, unless the singles bought. Most were attractive young women, but young men with the gift of the gab were also used. The most skilled of them could, in less than three minutes, make you believe they were your best and only friend.

Beyond where the bus had parked there was only a single, lonely stretch of road snaking up through the umbrella pines. The resort was isolated from the local transport system, and once inside there was no escape. The ups discovered the condition of their receiving the prize was that they had to stay an hour – more than enough time for them to be plied with strong drink, primed by the sizzlers, then tucked up by the closers.

Over by the side of the road, I could just make out a couple of young men in tan suits who had the clean-cut look of off-duty cruise-ship entertainers; these, I presumed, were the closers. By Spanish law, the timeshare companies had to allow a fourteen-day cooling-off period, so a prospective buyer could soberly reconsider his decision. But the ups never knew this, and by the time the closers got them round to signing the contract and credit-card slip –

the 'button-up' – they were too far gone on the punch to know what was happening.

I had seen old men crying like babies afterwards at the seafront cafes at what they had done; but in their way, the closers were as much victims of the system as the ups. They were working twelve-hour shifts in the season, commission-only, and they could only keep that up on cocaine or amphetamines provided by a house dealer. Eventually they ended up needing the long shifts just to cover their drug bills. Once they had worked in timeshare, no respectable business would take them on, so they were trapped, and the management effectively owned them.

As the closers began noticing our scrutiny, Mascarenas moved out of their sightline and led us up a concrete stair-way that smelt of cats and stale pee (clearly not intended to be seen by the ups) and across an astro-turf lawn to a bar. A trio of women in their mid-thirties wearing resort name-tags, who all looked as if they had been beauty con-testants in a former life, were seated at one end. As the barman was busy reaching for the bottles of grenadine and curaçao to mix a series of gaudy drinks with salacious names, Mascarenas put it to me that if I invested in the takeover of the resort as a director, I would enjoy privi-leged access to the most attractive sizzlers and OPCs. He gave me a stagey wink, and gestured towards the girls sit-ting at the bar.

The off-duty sizzlers were all dressed in outfits that

were chain-store versions of that season's catwalk shows. Mascarenas pointed out one of the girls in particular who he said was the face of the resort, used for all publicity shots and promotional material. He told me with some pride that she had once been a hostess at Milady Palace, the top-end escort bar in Marbella, patronized by Saudi royalty in the summer. Wearing a pussy-bow blouse and a tight skirt, she sat fiddling with an armful of bangles as Mascarenas pulled up two chairs opposite her. He and Bosano were holidaymakers, he explained, who were interested in buying timeshare in the Calahonda area, and friends had recommended they take a look at the resort. He didn't consider anything less than two weeks a proper holiday, and since he was also planning to buy a fortnight each for both of his two adult children by a previous marriage, he was prepared to buy a total of six weeks.

Mascarenas had introduced himself as every sizzler's dream, but the girl looked as uninterested at the end of his spiel as she had at the beginning and I began to wonder if our cover, such as it was, had been blown. At the end of the room I had noticed a large man leaning over the bar, talking loudly with all the confidence of a young lord; crowded around him were four girls in spangled dresses with plunging necklines. This, Bosano explained, was the current owner, Darren Canley, a former club promoter with a bad reputation, and an associate of Goldfinger Palmer, the Timeshare baron.

When one of the girls turned round, I could see that she was no more than eighteen years old. I noticed how unsteady she was on her heels as she laughed in unison with the other girls at Canley's patter. Although he wasn't looking in my direction, I sensed Canley had seen me, and I was feeling increasingly uncomfortable with the situation. There was no reasonable explanation for my being there: worse still, I knew Canley had dealt ecstasy in Ibiza, which meant it was likely he had worked either for Purse or with Purse's permission. Though I had no intention of coming in with Bosano and Mascarenas, when they showed their hand by bidding for the resort it would undoubtedly emerge that they had previously cased the joint, and it would be remembered by Canley that I had been with them. Given all the recent tensions, it was the sort of problem that I could have done without.

Drifting upstairs, I found an interview session for sizzlers being held. I tried to mingle as inconspicuously as possible, but the room was crammed only with women, the sort who would not have looked out of place at Milady Palace, and there were no men present. In fact, as I learned later, men were never interviewed as sizzlers, not even gay men. The women were all filling in forms and queuing to have their photos taken with a Polaroid camera. Overseeing the whole process was a heavily built matron type behind a desk. The questions she was asking related more to appearance than qualifications: it seemed the company was more interested in knowing about the height and weight of their applicants than in their academic achievements or recent work experience. Most of the women looked like ageing models who might need to subsidize their incomes, and exuded the curdled glamour characteristic of years working the clubs.

There were a few brief questions about their linguistic abilities, not unlike an oral examination at school; the rest was taken up with a series of role-play scenarios. The interviewers played a couple of retirees, anxious not to squander their limited capital, and the candidate had to reassure them they would be able to pay by instalments over an extended period, with post-dated cheques or credit card. If that didn't persuade them, they were offered the option of a loan organized by the company. At this point, the interviewers suddenly changed character, becoming a hostile pair of Scousers, and the emphasis was now on the candidate's ability to control difficult situations, to evaluate whether the pair were a lost cause, or could be talked round. As the touts often cheated the system by sending friends to the complex in order to be paid more commissions (as these were paid if the prospective customers stayed for an hour), the sizzlers could waste a lot of time trying to extract deposits from people who had no intention of buying: so extraction of the deposit was essential, since most ups could be expected – irrationally – to find the extra £5,000 necessary to complete their purchase, rather than lose their down payment.

Finally, we got out of there and were taken in the bus back to Elviria. I told Bosano I would be away in England for several weeks, and would let him know my decision about investing on my return. He looked somehow encouraged by this, as if my involvement was already a done deal, and I wondered uneasily if I should have signalled my lack of interest more clearly.

25

I had lied to Bosano about returning to England. In fact, with Purse no longer such an active threat after our talk, I remained at the chalet, avoiding Bosano's calls and not going out much for fear of running into him. I didn't want to tell him explicitly that I wasn't interested in the resort, for fear he would no longer help over Elisabeth, who I was still convinced we would find alive. There was no further news about her, nor any more contact from Purse, and I began to feel myself drifting again. I was smoking more marijuana than usual – a source I had found locally for Pakistani, rather than the usual Moroccan, would deliver to the lane – and it was making me lazy: in the afternoons I just watched old videos and worked my way through the last of the powder Jacobs had sent. Just a trip down to the *padel* bar or the beach felt like a major expedition.

One morning I rose late, as usual hungover and bleary, to see a battered VW Combi parked outside with Mark Hadley sitting at the wheel. The last time I had seen Hadley was in early '98, when he had helped me look for

Antar. I'd not heard from him in the intervening year, and had no idea what he'd been doing. He had the full ecstasy-Jesus thing going on now – his hair down to his shoulders, a lot of beads over a bare chest – and he looked nervous. 'Come for a drive with me,' he said when I invited him in. He was smiling, but there was something in his voice that suggested urgency.

I hesitated, reluctant to risk running into Bosano without good reason. 'Where? What's going on?'

'Not far.' He gestured vaguely to the west, in the direction of the coast road. 'Need to show you something.'

I agreed, but I must have looked dubious, as he seemed at pains to put me at ease and kept smiling encouragingly.

Our progress in his van was slowed by all the summer-holiday kids backing up the traffic at the turn-downs to the beaches. Hadley didn't say much as he drove. We passed the Kempinski Hotel, Las Dunas beach, then Ocean beach, and went up onto the new toll road. At the low-rise resort of Manilva, he turned off into the small industrial estate at the start of the ascent to Gaucín. There was a row of garages right by the road. Some were being used as scooter repair shops, there was a board shop at the end, and the air was heavy with the scents of hashish and motor oil. At the end of the row Hadley pulled up, and we got out. More slowly than was necessary, and not without an air of theatricality, he unfastened the single rusty padlock securing the garage nearest the road. Then, flinging the metal door upwards, he stood back to let me look inside.

I stepped forward, peering into the shadows. It took me a few moments to understand what I was seeing. About twenty-five crates were piled to the ceiling. None looked as if they had been opened. All were marked with Bowen's art courier logo, and they were covered in a fine patina of dust.

It was one of those rare moments when you genuinely wonder whether you're dreaming – I could scarcely believe my eyes, and actually felt dizzy with shock. My first, instinctive response was one of mild panic at how exposed we were. Kids were whizzing past behind us on scooters, glancing across as they went, and some nearby surfers were looking in our direction. 'Shut it, for God's sake! Shut the door!' I hissed at Hadley. He lowered it quickly.

My first thought was that Jim Dale, the sacked courier company employee, might have visited the gallery warehouse in Acton the night before we had gone there together, and that somehow Hadley had ended up with everything; but Hadley insisted this was not the case. Admittedly, the dust covering the crates seemed to go against it too; although I knew there were special-effects firms which made snow and dust for the film industry, and it was just about conceivable that Dale had a line through to Hadley, as he had been a friend of Bowen's.

But such a subterfuge seemed pretty unlikely, and

Hadley's explanation, initially at least, made a lot more sense. He told me that Bowen had laid gear on him for use at the free raves he organized around Granada, and one time he had followed Bowen back to his lab in the hills; so when Bowen died, he knew where to look. When the rumours about the Moroccans taking Bowen's gear started doing the rounds, he had finally felt safe enough to put his head above the parapet. Whether any of this was true or not, it was what Hadley was sticking to. When I tried to question him further, he just clammed up.

Maybe I should have paused more to wonder what was going on, as there were things that did not add up. Purse had told me that Drake was the one with Bowen's gear, but Drake's gear had been powder, and it had been in Zurich. Also, if the gear was in Spain all the time, then it was strange that Drake had moved some to Zurich – I could think of no reason why he should have. It seemed unlikely, but just about possible, that the gear had been stashed in different locations. Another oddity was that the crates contained pills, not powder; so if Purse was right about Drake, then it looked as if the material had been in different states when Bowen had died, or had been pressed since. Again, this was unusual, but not unheard of; and in the excitement of the moment, I was not going to let such matters stand in the way. After over a year of searching for it, I was looking at Bowen's stash. I felt my fingertips tingle as I began to work out how we would get it to where it needed to be.

My immediate priority was to move everything to a safer place. I chose a local courier company to take three crates at a time, and we loaded them up around the corner, out of sight of the garages. The company's vans were commonplace on the roads, and were less likely to be pulled than Hadley's camper or anything else we could have obtained at short notice. The stash was so large that it took two days and nine separate runs to get everything over to a cargo depot in Guadalhorce near Malaga airport. The units there were widely spaced out, and with all the comings and goings around the terminals, our activities attracted little attention.

At this time of year, with tens of thousands of holiday-makers flooding in for the pre-millennium summer parties, this was an area where the police already had their hands full. They would be unlikely to have time for any spot checks, as they did around the coastal roads. Only a couple of blocks away was the main prostitution drag; this was owned by the white girls in the daytime, and the Africans at night. When the police did enter the area it was mainly in response to complaints by the residents about the girls, or to take pay-offs from pimps. From the depot back to the chalet was only a forty-minute drive, through the hills and along the toll road, which also made it more accessible if we needed to move stock at short notice. I had expected some resistance from Hadley to relocating every-thing, but he appeared happy to go along with what I suggested.

On the way back from the depot on that second night, after we had everything stored, I finally tried out a couple of the pills. They were approximately 130 milligrams each, which made them about a third larger than cur-rent market produce, and as MDMA worked on body weight, this was encouraging. Each was enteric-coated, which suggested that Bowen or whoever had pressed them had used a top-end machine, perhaps from the pharma-ceutical or catering industries. The coating preserved the powder inside, but like any pharmaceutical, MDMA began deteriorating about five years from manufacture if not stored correctly. Although the containers had all been sealed with several layers of plastics, I was apprehensive about whether the pills would still work, but I needn't have worried: the buzz still felt almost as smooth and true as the buzz from fresh product.

The next morning Hadley came round looking dishev-elled, as if he had also been dipping hard in overnight. He cut up some of the pills on a plate and snorted them straight up into his bloodstream, coating and all. This was a common way ecstasy dealers demonstrated confidence in the purity of their produce, but as I had already tried the pills, it was rather superfluous. He insisted on it in any case. He was offering me a two-way split, on condition I bore the operating costs and that my old dope contacts in the States, Jamie Roth and Michael Pringle, were used as buyers. This was shrewd on his part: Roth and Pringle, having diversified into ecstasy in the late eighties, were now only one tier below Royal on the network, and could move over a million pills a week directly into the commercial rave scene. This put them among the small club of dealers who had the capacity to soak up a major consignment quickly.

Perhaps again at this point I should have wondered how Hadley knew about Pringle and Roth; but my immediate concern was that Hadley wanted everything done within two months, which seemed much too quickly given the preparations that were needed. I held out for four, so we could blend in with the boats returning for the winter season in the Caribbean. Hadley did not like this. He made it clear that if the goods were not shipped within that time, I would be out of the deal. Maybe, again, I should have been more worried about his insistence on this; but my focus at this stage was on making the deal work rather than putting up obstacles.

The next day Paul Jacobs flew down from London to join us, along with two of the couriers from the Zurich scam, Jon Piper and Gideon Roncelles. Immediately they began researching small charter boats and packaging. Dennis Watkins' old partner, Philip Han, was also on the team, agreeing to handle the Customs pay-offs and front companies.

The biggest snag was that Hadley wanted a minimum price per unit of ninety cents, and this was just not achievable at our sort of volume. The only two countries where over eighty cents could still be realized wholesale were the US and Australia, but only for deals in the tens of thousands: for anything larger than that it was closer to seventy, and Australian margins were about 30 per cent higher than the US. Hadley's figure was not realistic regardless of the quality, but I reckoned this was just because he was accustomed to pricing from deals in the thousands and had never dealt in the bulk market, and so hoped that I would be able to talk him round once we had some projections.

Integral to making these projections was Philip Han, as he had a good working relationship with Jakarta customs. If we could fly product direct from Madrid, he could get everything to Kupang on East Timor, and from there into the regular people-smuggling route to the Northern Territories of Australia. He had used the route only a few months previously without problems. For all this, his fee was only $100,000 and 10 per cent of the gross. This option gave us reasonable returns, certainly better than anything we could have got from the US option. Unfortunately, Hadley would not hear of anything except the American route, and despite my explaining that prices always dropped for deals over 10,000 units, he was stubbornly sticking to his price.

We spent a couple of days pacing in the chalet, trying to square this circle, but Hadley was no longer responding to any arguments rationally. He was taking pills every day, snorting powder and wandering about in a daze. No one knew who he was meeting when he was not at the chalet, or how much loose talk was going on, and he had been seen several times down at the beach in his Jesus gear, handing out pills. Finally, losing patience with all this, Jacobs pressed to move five crates by the Australian route without telling Hadley. If it worked, we would move more that way, and keep Hadley's share as if it came from Roth and Pringle – if it failed, the loss would be soaked up by my share of the American deal. Han's up-front fee was to come from the second half of the Zurich scam, which we would now use to fund the bigger scam. I knew Jacobs would walk if I did not agree, but I needed him. So, reluctantly, I agreed, and took the evening flight from Malaga to Zurich to prepare.

26

Before arriving in Zurich in late June I left a message for Drake telling him, without getting into specifics, that I wanted to switch routes and buyers. After a week there was no response, and when I left more messages at his Little Venice flat and in Madrid, there was still no reply. As time was short, I decided not to delay further and to move ahead as planned, and I vowed to send him his cut once the deal had gone through.

The Germans from Hamburg, whose dog had almost been used first time around, were already waiting for me. They came to the same Zoo Dolder apartment we had used the previous time for the packaging. We no longer had to wait for the skiing season, as this time, powder for 250,000 pills was being sent by a mailshot technique that I had used for small deliveries in the past, and the other half we were going to deal directly into raves to up returns and ensure we had enough to cover all the operational costs of the Hadley scam. Several new holiday cottages had again been rented for cash in the flat fields of East

Anglia, and three packages – slim and supple enough to fit through the letterboxes, so not requiring a delivery office pick-up – were sent to each cottage. By the end of the week, we had all but one of the packages, and were ready to get started with the pressing. For increased security measures we avoided going to the cottage that had been due to receive the missing package.

We watched the rest of the cottages carefully, but after three weeks there were no signs of surveillance at any of the remaining addresses, and so the pressing machine was moved in. This time we used proper charcoal filter masks to avoid getting high in the pressing process. The press head fitted, and we used ascorbic acid and magnesium stearate as fillers to stop the machine jamming or chucking out powder. The pills were dropped to Salomon at the car park, without incident or Purse wanting to see me in person again. The next day we began pushing Drake's share of the cash through a number of bureaux de change in central London. So far, so good.

An Egyptian who owned several bureaux near the Edgware Road was known to handle such transactions for a reasonable fee. Several other bureaux around Queensway, run by Egyptians and Israeli Arabs, also did business of this sort. There had long been talk that they were grasses, since that was the only reasonable way to stay in the business, but I had never had any problems with them in the past. In a further push to save time, we did everything through them. The bureaux wired it all through at intervals and in small packets to Drake's Gibraltar accounts – he had one of those set-ups wherein several company accounts were owned by a blind trust, which was in turn owned by another company. No one knew what international payments triggered a red flag, and the rules changed all the time. For a while, £10,000 was the bar, but that had been reduced, and the safest way was to break the payments up and spread them around as much as possible. In the event, all went through without a hitch. I flew back to Zurich, praying that the wind was finally behind us.

Then, while Hadley's attention was diverted (he thought they were looking at a boat in Alicante), Jacobs, Roncelles and Piper came up to the Zoo Dolder apartment to help with the rest of the pilling. As the remaining 250,000 were to be encapsulated rather than pressed, this was a slower process. The encapsulating machines were hand-operated and only delivered twenty-four pills at a time. This meant that everyone had to sit round a small hill of powder with the charcoal masks on, digging out the batches like children playing in a sandpit.

Jacobs had also brought more worrying news about Hadley. He was continuing his pill handouts at the beach, and had been pulled in by the police while wandering about stoned in a park in Marbella Nueva. Nothing had happened, but I was anxious to get back and try to put a lid on this, so when the encapsulation was finished we did not take a breather. Roncelles and Piper went to pick up three cheap vans for cash from separate pitches on the outskirts, to use to cross into Spain that weekend. One of the vans looked vaguely respectable; the other two needed to be the lowest, most dishevelled vehicles available, and would serve as decoys going ahead through the border controls (such as they were). In a city like Zurich, where everyone was superficially law-abiding, it proved difficult to find vehicles that looked sufficiently scruffy. We ended up having to bash them around a bit and smear dirt on them ourselves.

We filled all three vans with items from a Chinese wholesaler out near the airport: T-shirts, whistles, baseball caps, all items that could plausibly be sold at a rave. We planned to pay off the door staff and go in as local vendors, selling the pills at almost retail prices to the dealers on the floor.

The pills were triple-packed in thick plastic, the packs hosed down, and then they were loaded into the spare tyre and axle bars of the rear van. Normally, crossing internal borders in Europe, we might not have bothered with this, but the Swiss border was an unpredictable one. Switzerland was not part of the Schengen open-border system, and checks were still performed there regularly. Officers had to be seen to be responding to complaints by EC states that cash was continually being transported away from their fiscal systems into Swiss accounts. Theoretically this meant their attention was on inward traffic; but Customs can stop any vehicle they do not like the look of, often on a system of precedent which is not entirely rational and impossible to predict. If a white van with certain plates has yielded a haul in the past, similar vehicles will then get pulled in perpetuity. So we had to plan for the worst and make the vans as check-proof as possible.

This time I drove in front as a decoy, with Jacobs and Roncelles following and Piper last. All three vans got through without attracting any attention. Eight hours later we were in Barcelona at a giant rave in a sculpture park, and by the end of the event, we had already moved about 30,000 pills to the dealers on the floor and had taken in over £50,000 cash, in mixed currencies, mainly pesetas. The following morning we boarded the ferry for Ibiza without further delay in Barcelona. I had a legitimate reason for being on the island, which would work as a cover of sorts, and we had timed our visit accordingly – the time had come for me to take up my writer-in-residence post at Manumission for three weeks, along with Kris Needs and Irvine Welsh. The plan now was to move the remaining pills during my residency. While Mike McKay and Claire Davies put me up at the Pink Pussy Motel in Jesus, the others decamped to Pike's Hotel outside San Antonio.

Pike's was set in tropical gardens which had been

used as the set for Wham's 'Club Tropicana' video in the eighties, and as the backdrop for several extravagant Queen parties in the same period. Now it had fallen on hard times and was almost empty. We planned to use it to hold the gear, and for meets with the house dealers when they got up, which was usually about three in the afternoon.

My memories of the island were hazy. I had first visited with a group of fellow Oxford stoners in the sixties, and that trip was just a blur: all I had retained was an image of some draft-dodgers waking up to find they had camped on a level crossing. I had come again in '73 while on the run from the British police, as Spain and Britain did not have a working extradition treaty at this time, but I had mostly stayed indoors then. My most recent visit – to Manumission, within the past year – was also just a blur as there had been ecstasy on tap from the moment I had touched down, and I did not really have a sense of the geography of the place or how best to move from one town to the next. But on the way in I had looked at maps and guidebooks to get a feel for the place, and after the success of the Barcelona deal, my hope was that as long as we could get into the raves we would be able to sell fast.

Driving round in the van that first day, the only things that looked familiar were the strips in Jesus, Ibiza Town and San Antonio, and the Cafe del Mar, the famous chill-out lounge on the seafront which I had visited the previous year. It occurred to me that I had never really seen the island in daylight nor in an un-intoxicated state before, so this lack of familiarity was hardly surprising. This time, I intended to keep a clearer head.

I attended Manumission on Monday nights at Privilege to write my pieces on the scene there while Jacobs connected with the floor dealers. The club turned over at least a million pounds' worth of MDMA every Monday night, and we hoped to move 80,000 units of our stock in the three-week period, at almost retail prices, from five to ten pounds per unit if we could get away with that, depending on the time of night and the level of demand.

One reason for Manumission's popularity was that it featured live hardcore sex acts involving dwarves, vampires and porn stars which the audience were encouraged to participate in, and these guaranteed a heaving floor from about one in the morning onwards. I was determined not to take anything while in the club, so I could keep an eye on things, but this proved more difficult than I expected as half the drinks passed to me were laced with liquid ecstasy, acid or MDMA. The only way to stay straight was to order a drink, pour out the contents and replace them with something one had brought in. But although this is what I did, strangely I still felt I was getting high in the club, and could hardly focus on anything. Some weirdos with their bodies painted like zebras were wandering around, blowing bubbles and throwing confetti; I reckoned what they were blowing was probably laced with something, and I kept out of their slipstream as best I could and felt somewhat better for it.

It seemed at that point, July '99, as if every crazy kid from around the world was converging on the island. In a few months it was to be the new millennium, and all the shops were selling editions of Nostradamus; on billboards all over the island was his prediction that 'in the Seventh month of Nineteen-ninety-nine the great King of Terror will come from the sky', and a lot of the people looked as if they weren't waiting to find out if this was going to happen. They were partying like it was already the end. The motel was awash with pole dancers, dwarves and vampires, all off their heads and having sex in public. In the toilet booths, a famous stage dwarf called Johnny Golden was attempting to force-feed the dancers with vodka, and through the windows one could see people dressed in orange robes, kneeling with bowed heads or staring at the sky.

I tried to keep my eyes down on the numbers. About 5,000 pills were going out to various dealers across the island every day, but not always as belly-to-belly deals, and this rate was too slow: we were wasting time chasing up debts when we should have been selling. Although our pills were better than anything on the island, this wasn't being reflected in the prices. We had to sell cheaper and focus on cash deals in the clubs, as it was obvious that the dealing scene on the island was completely bombed out, a free-for-all in the worst sense. The market was at rock bottom for the dealer, and perfect for the punter. I had expected something bad, but only in the middle of all the chaos, standing among the carnage, did one get a real sense of how bad it was and why the place was no longer a cash cow for Purse. It was only too clear why he wanted to get into the more profitable and predictable American market.

In that market – which was still structured and hierarchical, and also much larger – the first-in advantage still prevailed for Juan Royal and his network. He had established contacts with all the big rave and club organizers well before anyone else was in the game, and he sat on top of the vast system like the king of the castle. If second-tier suppliers like Roth or Pringle wanted to sell on any scale, they had to use Royal's network and kick back to him some of their profits for the privilege, or else sell some of his gear alongside their own. Independent small-town suppliers existed, of course, but because of the scale of the market and the difficulty in obtaining precursor chemicals, their reach was limited. Royal effectively had a loose monopoly over the most profitable ingestible substance by weight on the planet.

By contrast, in Europe, the only comparable market for scale, the scene was chaotic and unregulated. Chemicals were not as difficult to obtain, and Dutch labs and

Vietnamese gangs were prolifically knocking out budget product. As new clubs and raves popped up all the time, anyone could chance their hand dealing there.

At that moment, Ibiza felt to me like it was at the epi-centre of this decline. In the eighties, over 90 per cent of the distribution on the island had been fronted by the local Spanish gypsy gangs, and the same condition applied to other islands like Mallorca and many of the mainland resorts. To clean up, all Purse had to do was ensure his relations with the gypsy bosses stayed tight, and that he kept them supplied with good standardized product that no one complained about. But it was not long before his dominance was being eroded, as local urban dealers began coming south for the summer and bringing cheaper-grade pills to finance their holidays. The story went round that in the early days of 1990–91, one week you could be sign-ing on at the dole office in Manchester, the next driving down from Rotterdam with a boot full of pills, and the week after that driving home in a Ferrari. The gold rush was on, and every two-bit dealer in Northern Europe was converging on Spain over the summer to sell his wares. Prices and quality plummeted.

To make matters worse, at around this time much-feared and respected firms like the Adams family from North London had also elbowed in on raves and clubs across the island selling the cheaper Brink's-Mat gear, which had taken over like a virus. The small army of flyer distributors, constantly patrolling the beaches and bars handing out invites to the club nights, were also in on the action, and had been expanding their operations up to the present day, freebooting more of the cheap Brink's-Mat pills from the house dealers. Now everyone getting off a flight seemed to have some pills to sell, and it had got to the point where there were more dealers than punters. One morning during just a five-minute walk in the old town, I was pitched over a dozen times.

So when I met up with the others at the Bar Jamaica in Ibiza Town, I told them we had to get realistic and slash prices. Apart from one photograph of the Jamaican football team, the bar was just a typical Spanish bar: lottery results blared from a television in the corner. It was about the most low-key place we could find and everyone was looking dazed and demoralized, even though we had converted 30,000 pills into over £70,000 cash, mostly in pesetas, after expenses. Even Jacobs, who was wearing a ridiculous Hawaiian shirt and looking like a nerd on holiday, seemed in low spirits. It was obvious the island had already taken its toll on us, and we needed to be pragmatic and minimize our remaining time there – whatever the cost. Otherwise, we simply would not be up to doing the run of Hadley's stash of the Bowen pills to the Northern Territories.

We all agreed that only late at night, when people began running low at the clubs, was there anything like a demand situation we could work with. We had to stick to the clubs, not waste time trying to sell to outside distributors. So the door staff at Manumission and Ministry were paid off again, and the sell to the floor dealers was repeated. It took us about a further week to offload the remainder of the stock, and we got about a third less net overall than planned. Then the two older vans were abandoned in a car park in Ibiza Town, and while Piper drove the newer van back the rest of us split up and took separate flights back to Malaga. It had all taken less time than any of the other deals I had worked on since getting out of prison, and had been considerably more lucrative.

27

In my experience, the banks around Marbella were not unaccustomed to seeing large amounts of cash being wired from their tills, and I did not anticipate any significant problems transferring Philip Han's handling fee. Jacobs had some old empty passports and driving licences where the details had to be printed in; these would not have passed muster at an airport, but they were sufficient as ID for banks. We split Han's £100,000 into five packages and sent them from Barclays, Guadalmina Alta, the Banco Popular in Nueva Andalucia and three more branches of the Banco Popular down the coast to Calahonda. None of the till staff at any of the branches so much as raised an eyebrow.

Meanwhile, Jacobs was preparing the five crates for the trip to Jakarta and was looking for cargo – ideally, some industrial samples – that was being returned pre-packaged to a sender in Jakarta. I knew from my time in Pakistan and Thailand in the seventies that this tended to be a safer way of using air freight, as the packages would already have acquired customs stamps from the earlier journey: they had already been logged on the computers and processed, and if the weight was the same, they tended to attract less attention on their return journey. Unfortunately, we couldn't find anything of that size being returned.

The route we were taking into Asia was not as unproblematic as it first appeared. Although Jakarta flights had sometimes been used as a route for heroin from Burma and the Triangle into Europe, and common sense suggested the choke point would be on inbound flights, most of the heroin imported to Europe was now Afghan and the Asian product went to the States. As Spain was increasingly becoming a drug trans-shipment hub, it was just as likely that something might have been going out to the Asian market than the reverse. The reality was that any goods from Spain were now suspect, and with good reason. As Spanish Customs were not as lackadaisical and corrupt as in the old days, there was a real risk our gear would not get off the ground unless we were careful.

We toyed with using another European airport: Schiphol had many more direct flights to Jakarta due to the colonial connections between Holland and Indonesia, and there was probably going to be less heat on that route. But when I put this to Han, he felt we should not delay things in case there were shift changes his end. He sounded a little less sure of himself, so I did not want to push him. Instead, we all focused on making the Spanish route work as safely as possible.

Our research had showed that a type of Spanish nougat known as *turrón* had been shipped from Madrid to Jakarta in the preceding months: this was a product that had been exported to neighbouring countries from the Philippines for some decades, but upmarket outlets in the area apparently preferred the original Spanish product. We opted for a straightforward camouflage job; the pills were repackaged using the genuine nougat boxes, and to the casual eye, the boxes, letterheads and waybills of our consignment looked identical to those of the earlier shipments. Only the phone numbers were changed, so that in the event of any comeback the calls would be routed to phones we controlled.

There was still one problem, however. If anything did not look right on X-ray or raised suspicion, customs officers usually opened crates for inspection at the point where there was already a lid of some sort. They did this simply because they did not want the bother of repackaging, and they looked under the first layers of whatever was inside to see if anything was hidden. Only the most dedicated did more than that, or punched holes in the side. Consequently, smugglers liked using deep crates and placing their items in layers beneath the standard search range. Our problem was that our crates were not particularly deep, and to change them would mean altering the look of the nougat consignment which Jacobs had already carefully prepared.

It is on such technical points that a scam can succeed or fail, and there was something of a stand-off – Piper and Roncelles arguing that crates come in all sizes, and going deeper was not going to draw attention to the consignment, but Jacobs saying that the nougat had been going through regularly for months, officers would be used to the look of it, that the dimensions of the crates might already be computer logged and anything different could raise a red flag. Smuggling is all about managing risk and variables, but as in life, these can never be eliminated completely. I could see both sides of the argument.

Meanwhile, the nougat from the boxes was piling up in the chalet and melting in the heat, its sickly sweet smell getting into everything. Tempers were getting frayed and time was being lost. So as not to delay any further, I suggested we kept things as they were. The next day the crates were couriered up to the cargo terminal in Barajas for the onward flight, but almost immediately, things went wrong. Han was on the phone saying his officers had not been in the right place when the crates came in, and he was refusing to take any blame, saying we had held off too long. He now needed another $50,000 for more payoffs to get the crates back to Barajas.

Within an hour, the money was wired through; but the next day, there were no crates on the flight. Han's story was that the money had not reached him. I faxed proof of the transfer and we were promised them for the following day, but nothing came. Roncelles was at a hotel up in Barajas with the van, waiting to bring everything back, but five days later he was still waiting. I kept phoning Han, and he kept assuring me everything was in hand. Adding to the rising temperature was Hadley, who was coming round every day in a state to the chalet, wanting to know what the delay was and wanting to see the boat.

When I got onto Han again, a week behind schedule, he promised the crates would be on that day's flight. He said he needed $20,000 more, and I told him that would be the last payment. But within minutes Hadley was round in a fury: he had been down to Guadalhorce, and seen the five crates had gone. I told him there had been a security scare, that we had begun moving crates back to Manila and it had been a false alarm. He wanted to check, so I had to agree to meet him there that evening.

The moment Hadley had gone I told Roncelles to bring everything down on the Talgo fast train from Atocha station, then hire a van when he arrived. It was the only way he had a chance of making it – but Hadley was waiting when I arrived, and he looked tense. He did not have the key anymore, but he was pulling on the shutters to the lock-up and had almost got them open. I had no idea whether Roncelles had made it in time. Slowly I unrolled the door, praying, but it was empty inside.

Hadley went very pale and looked as if he was about to go for me, but just at that moment Roncelles swung around the corner. His story was that he had been told to bring the crates back to the depot, but halfway there had realized that we were meeting at the garage, so had come back. Gradually Hadley relaxed; when he saw all the nougat boxes, he did not like it, but we told him that had just been an extra measure for the security scare. The relief of seeing the five crates was so overwhelming that he seemed about to cry.

To get Hadley off our backs, we spent the next few days looking for a boat for the American route so that we could show it to him and he could see things were moving as planned. Han was also in touch again; he was keen not to lose his 10 per cent, and offering to set up a receiving company in the Bahamas without further charge. This would be a swimming-pool cleaning outfit, a common cover for drug scams due to the chemicals that could be ordered legitimately by such companies; but it had become too common a cover, in my opinion. What with everything else that had gone on, my confidence in Han had now expired. Instead I asked Roth to handle the receiving company.

As Roth and Pringle always worked with Mexican runners out of Tijuana, specifically with Teo Hernandez of the Sinaloa cartel, this was an old and well-oiled relationship. The goods were coming in on the east coast, near Cancun, and travelling overland before crossing the border near Calexico. As this journey was far outside the territory of Hernandez, the work would have to be sub-contracted to another Mexican firm. Roth had assured me we would not be losing control at that point, as Hernandez was feared throughout northern Mexico, and Roth would have his own people monitoring the sub-contractors. However, I knew from my own bitter experience that Americans monitoring Mexicans always led to trouble, and everyone tried to think of a way to ease this situation without making the Mexicans feel under pressure. In the end it was decided the crew would also be present at the handover. As it turned out, the problem (there always is one) would come from an entirely different direction, and be of a nature I could not possibly have anticipated.

For the moment, everything progressed calmly. The boat we found was moored ten kilometres down the coast at Puerto Duquesa, one of the quieter marinas favoured by owners who did not want to pay the exorbitant berthing rates at Banus or Estepona. The boat was chartered for four weeks at post-season rates, and we negotiated an itinerary: our own crew would make the crossing, and the regular crew would board once the goods had been offloaded. The swimming-pool company front was abandoned, as the Mexicans, accompanied by Roth's people and our crew, would now meet our boat with their own launch. They would transfer everything overland in a fruit truck to one of the well-trodden border crossings near Calexico.

Once he saw the boat, Hadley was no longer on our case, and by early October 1999, everything was more or less in place. A crew had been hired, former associates of Dennis Watkins', who was still missing, all experienced single men who knew the risks involved, and apart from some minor engine trouble, the crossing went smoothly. Roth's men were there with the Mexicans, as arranged. There was no funny business at the handover, and the crew decamped to Cancun to unwind.

From now on, there was nothing more I could do. The operation was in the lap of the gods, and we just had to sit patiently. For the first time in several months, I slept soundly. The following morning, I packed my bags and set out on a trip that would end two days later in Darmstadt – home of my German editor, Marcus – where a three-day millennial rave was already getting underway.

28

I headed first to London, and from there I would go on to a parade in Berlin, where I had been invited to DJ, then fly straight on to Darmstadt. If everything went well, and once the post-scam heat had died down, I planned to go on to La Vileta to see the family to unwind over the autumn and into the New Year. My intention was to distract myself as much as possible from what was going on in Mexico, and on the flight from Malaga to London I tried to relax and banish all thoughts of the operation from my mind. I downed several vodkas and stared out of the window, attempting to lose myself in the moment, but although I could not put my finger on why exactly, I was already unsettled by the Mexican deal. I had been here before, but the visions I had were properly apocalyptic this time. I could feel deep inside me that something was going to go badly wrong.

I would be DJing alongside Billy Idle at the Berlin rally; when I picked him up from his Ladbroke Grove flat early the next morning, he looked as if he hadn't slept, which made two of us. Our hosts, Timing Music's Armin and ET, were waiting for us at the other end, and within seconds of getting into their car, the interior had filled with thick white smoke. Idle started sweating. His Manchester patter was incomprehensible to the Germans, who thought he was complaining about the quality of their dope and pulled out some special buds and skinned those up.

It was strong – so strong, in fact, that temporarily my sense of hearing became radically distorted. Only an hour later I found myself in the front float of the procession, surrounded by 50,000 revellers, millennium fever gripping everyone already. There was a desperate craziness in people's eyes that I had never seen at such events before, and I thought back to all the dancers in Ibiza earlier that summer, wearing their Nostradamus prophecies. As we moved through the Brandenburg Gate, music blared from all sides so loudly that it was difficult to know how my selection of music registered. I was so tense that I played one track, 'Grow More Weed', twice, and everyone was so spaced out and gone they did not even seem to notice.

The next day, it was a changed-looking Marcus who met me at Frankfurt airport. He still had the dreadlocks, but now he wore a smart suit and looked as if he had stepped out of a men's fashion magazine: it was quite a transformation. Driving me in a new customized Mercedes van directly to his headquarters in Darmstadt, he told me he had invested the profits from the sales of the German

edition of my autobiography in a headshop in an upscale
shopping district. I was a little surprised, as I had lost
sight of what had been happening with the book. I knew
French, Spanish and Italian versions were selling steadily,
but it turned out the German sales had outstripped all
other foreign editions to such an extent that Marcus had
cleaned up.

I had never seen such an opulent headshop. The front
was taken up with a large selection of underground litera-
ture, and a giant rack of paperbacks of *Mr Nice*; the rest
was filled with top-end legal high products and every sort
of paraphernalia. There were digital scales, sunlamps,
grinders, microscopes to view trichome crystals on buds,
and special climate-controlled containers that held soil
nutrients and other growing aids. Pride of place was given
to a display of bongs and pipes. These were no ordinary
items: they were precision-made, encrusted with semi-
precious stones, many even gold- and silver-plated. They
started at around $200.

It was difficult to imagine how all this was tolerated by
the authorities. Usually headshops were sited in backstreets
and had blacked-out windows like porn shops, but this
was on a main shopping thoroughfare among expensive-
looking shops selling furs, jewellery and watches. The
front had been set up for me to sign books: a desk was piled
with more copies of *Mr Nice*, *Mr Nice* lighters, *Mr Nice*
smoking papers and *Mr Nice* bookmarks. There was a

long queue down the street. I had never seen anything like it. My head was swimming, and the shop was full of dope smoke so thick one could hardly see one's way around.

After the signing, Marcus drove us to a rave on the outskirts of the city. The event was held again at Krone, but it was unrecognizable from its first incarnation. It was a more out-of-control crowd, and as in Ibiza and Berlin, everyone seemed to have caught the millennial fever. Men with scars and a hard ghetto look mingled jubilantly with wide-eyed teens in surf shorts with their skin smeared with day-glo paint. Further in were crowds swarming over bouncy castles, helter-skelters and a mock Egyptian temple. Marcus had already told me he had a special batch of ecstasy made by the young chemists from Merck. He passed me some. It tasted bitter and was so strong that, unlike any I'd had before, the effect began coming on almost immediately. It was the purest I had ever encountered.

We made our way between a jostling mass of black and white peacocks, multi-coloured scarecrows and clowns in romper suits. Beyond, on a platform, were the dancers, but they seemed unable to dance: they appeared just to be screaming maniacs in outlandish costumes waving their arms in the air. At least, that was how they appeared until the pills fully kicked in: then their fingers and heads and legs seemed to be dancing to their own separate rhythms, their limbs pumping like frogs' legs being given electric jolts. I threw myself amongst them, losing track of time until a foghorn signalled the end of the revelry.

The music stopped abruptly, and the dance-floor emptied with surprising speed. As we staggered out looking for the van, the street was suddenly full of armed, uniformed cops. Already we were surrounded. I froze, and began futilely trying to empty my pockets of any remaining drugs. It was only too clear that we were off our heads, but worse, I was sure that this was linked to the operation. Someone had obviously talked, and while we had been inside my movements must have been traced from the airport.

But to my surprise the police ignored me, and focused on Marcus. There were some brief exchanges in German, which I could just about understand: it seemed the cops had traced the van registration to the headshop, and had been waiting for its owner to emerge. In the end, after searching only Marcus, they let us go. No offence as such had been committed, and it looked like harassment pure and simple. As we got into the van, Marcus brushed it off. 'They have nothing better to do than hassle me,' he said with a shrug. I hoped he was right. As abruptly as they had appeared, the police withdrew, and we drove off to find another party where we could dance off the drugs. It would turn out to be my last carefree night for some time.

29

Early the next morning, I got a call from Jacobs. He sounded anxious, and told me that one of the crew, Michael Barr, had returned from Cancun seriously unwell. I felt bad for him, but from an operational standpoint I was not concerned, as Barr's role was over and he had probably just picked up something nasty in Cancun. I told Jacobs to get Barr a doctor and to keep me informed, then tried to go back to sleep.

A few hours later Jacobs called again, telling me Barr's condition had deteriorated. And now there was more bad news: a friend of Barr's, Peter Isola, was also in a bad way. At this point Jacobs said that Barr had admitted passing Isola a few hundred pills he had filched from the boat, during the American crossing, and that he thought there was a problem with them. We were facing a potential catastrophe of many millions of dodgy pills hitting the American market.

Of course, everyone had tried samples without any problems. Hadley had been necking the pills for months and had not got sick, and I told Jacobs not to worry and to get the two men the best doctor he could. I suggested he use Charles Triay, a British-trained Gibraltarian, whose practice was in San Pedro de Alcántara, near at hand. As a precaution I also got him to send some pills to a lab in Barcelona for analysis, as this was a place Saunders and I had used to source our pill-testing kits and it was discreet.

At this point, I still felt reasonably relaxed. I was sure Bowen would never have put his name to moody gear. The overland crossing to Calexico had passed off without a hitch, and in a couple of days the goods would be across the border and the money would begin flowing back.

On arrival from Darmstadt at Malaga airport, I drove straight to the villa Jacobs had rented for looking after the two men, to check on things. It was in the Valle del Sol, round the back of Guadalmina Alta, one of those villas that only get used for a few weeks every summer and are empty the rest of the year. As I drove through those quiet backstreets looking for it, I began to feel the first stirrings of a more serious anxiety.

The drive was overgrown, the pool drained and full of leaves. Someone had locked the gates, and there was a car outside I did not recognize, but presumed it was that of the doctor. I rang the bell, and when no one answered, I climbed through the gate and walked down the drive. At the end was an old fountain that had stopped working; all the shutters were down and covered in dust and grime. It looked as if the place had not been occupied for years, and a smell of damp and decay came off everything. Standing there, I rang the doorbell; again no one answered, and at first no sounds came from within except a faint moaning which might have just been the wind but seemed to be coming from the back. It felt like one of those moments when one's whole world is about to rearrange itself in an order one no longer recognizes.

Walking round through the overgrown gardens, I found the men in a room at the rear. Both were in a much worse state than I had anticipated. Barr was suffering from tremors, and his left eye had closed over. He was weak and delirious. I had never seen anything like this before. Jacobs was wearing a mask, as was the doctor. He was a man I did not recognize – a Spaniard, not Triay – and he said an ambulance had already been ordered to come that evening and move the men to the Clinica in Marbella.

There was nothing more I could do there, so I drove straight round to Hadley's. It only took ten minutes, as there was a shortcut over the dry river at the back of Guadalmina to El Paraiso, where his bungalow was. His camper was there at the front, covered with sand blown in from the beach. The front door was open, but when I called there was no reply. His toiletries were gone from the bathroom, and some of his clothes, and it looked as if he had left in a hurry. I had to alert the American connection that something serious might be up.

When I phoned Roth, the goods were close to crossing the border, only a few miles away, and there was more bad news. Some of his people had got sick, and the symptoms sounded eerily similar to what I had just seen. This was the clincher as far as I was concerned: I knew his people would have been trying samples, so some link with the pills now seemed undeniable.

When I told Roth I thought the pills were bad, he sounded sceptical. I had the sense he would knock them out whatever I said and we would have a disaster on our hands, but I managed to get him to agree not to hand out more samples, and to hold the goods at the border for another day. Then I went back to the airport and got on a connecting flight via Barajas for Mexico City. It was a regular route with several flights daily, and that evening, local time, I was on another connecting flight to Tijuana.

Hernandez had sent some people to meet me. They were waiting when I arrived, and took me to a hotel on the main drag near the bullring, a block back from the beach. Hernandez did not come over in person – he was having some heat from the Federales due to some other unrelated shipments, which had been intercepted – but when I got in we spoke on the phone. The story I gave him was that I needed to get to the pills before they moved, to check for a bad batch. Hernandez did not seem particularly surprised: moving goods every week, he was probably used to such problems. I made clear everything was still technically mine, not Roth's, and I would settle all his logistical costs myself. He seemed satisfied with this.

After finishing the call, I bought paraffin and six charcoal masks from a builder's shop on Salido, then found an international phone call place back on the drag which stank of chilli. From there I put a call through to an old friend in the State Department in Washington, and then waited, and two hours later he called back with the news I had expected and feared.

My story about the bad batch had, in fact, been a misdirection. I was sure now that all the pills were bad, all except those Hadley had handed out from that one crate – lethal, in fact. I did not think I even needed to test them now to know that.

The next morning two of Hernandez's men came round in an Explorer, and we drove out into the desert. Great ridged storm clouds lay over the range the locals called the Sierra Escondida and over the arroyos further north. Tracks along the sides of these arroyos led us along the run-down outskirts of the border towns. Beyond an assortment of chicken farms and warehouses, on the eastern edge of Mexicali, a trail led on for an hour to a gully where two older men were waiting beside a truck. They had the look of men who had seen most things in their time. About a mile further – not clearly demarked from where we were, just looking like more scrubland – lay the US border.

All the goods were still in their fruit crates, and the scene seemed strangely peaceful, like the end of a long film when the whole story has been told except for the denouement. The men already knew what was about to happen, and there was no tension; everything unfolded as if in slow motion. The money left from the Zurich scam was still in pesetas in my pockets, but they knew its worth, about $20,000 in total, and took it and pulled down the crates, then put on the masks and stood well back. There were so many crates that the paraffin covered only half of them, but that was enough. The fire took quickly, and we stood and watched as the toxic smoke rose high in a funnel shape over the desert and merged with the sky.

Soon it would be the new millennium, and I wanted to be back with my daughters. Without returning to the hotel, I asked the men in the Explorer to drop me at the airport and took the first connecting flight to Europe. Twenty hours later I was at Palma airport; it was the middle of the night, local time. In a hire car, I headed for the house in La Vileta. I intended to avoid the route where I had passed the roadside Madonna, because I didn't want to be reminded of what had happened there, but somehow I found myself on that same road again. There had been a lot of construction work in the area, but it looked like the same place.

I couldn't help myself. I began looking out for the image. I was sure that fate had brought me to her again;

but the strange thing was that although I was certain I was in the same spot, the Madonna was nowhere to be seen. I drove round in circles to see if I could find somewhere else that looked the same, but there was nowhere. I wondered if it had been pulled down, or moved. All I could see in the same place on that dusty roadside was an image of a woman advertising a local wine. Her lips were full and sensual, her eyes knowing. She was gazing out over the Mallorcan hills possessively with those beautiful eyes, as if all her dreams would be fulfilled there. It had been dark when I had first passed the place, and perhaps I had been mistaken as to what I had seen.

30

Two months later, Nostradamus's predictions having passed without incident, I found myself in Agadir in southern Morocco. It had been years since I had last been there, and the place did not seem to have changed for the better. There was a Sofitel now one block back from the front, and other new resort hotels in a row next to it. Along the promenade were restaurants serving European food and several escort bars, the girls sitting outside looking overdressed and bored. The city had been destroyed by an earthquake in the middle of the twentieth century, and back from the front there was little of any architectural interest left: just hosed-down boulevards and nondescript backstreets that could have been anywhere.

I wandered about for a couple of days killing time, taking long walks along the windy beach and looking at the sardine fleet along the coast. I had no desire to arrive early for my rendezvous.

The recovery of Barr and Isola and Roth's people would be a slow process, but it now seemed assured. The

laboratory in Barcelona had confirmed that the crate
from which the initial samples had been drawn, along
with Hadley's supplies, had been clean. They had also confirmed the other pills had tested positive for toxins on the
enteric coating including antimony, nickel and mercury.
The pills I had brought back from Mexico had tested
exactly the same, and it seemed certain now that everything except Hadley's crate had been contaminated by the
time it reached the boat and probably long before that.

Royal, who it turned out was the original client of the
pills, had told Purse that the consignment had fallen into
the wrong hands, and apparently he had known what he
was talking about. If it had gone to market it would have
resulted in the worst case of ecstasy-related hospitalization
ever. This had been avoided by a matter of hours, since
once they had crossed the border I wouldn't have got to
them since I was persona non grata in the US. Thousands
would have become sick and died if the pills had reached
the market, and Royal had every reason to prevent that
from happening, so there were no repercussions. It would
have taken the ecstasy business a generation to recover
after a disaster like that, and it was a business he had virtually founded – the only business he knew.

As to how the toxins got there in the first place, the
Barcelona lab had said the contamination was consistent
with exposure to certain pesticides, but more likely it had
come from exposure to an area where industrial metals

were being worked – a smelting yard, for example. They couldn't be more specific than that. Whatever the source, we were all extremely fortunate, and we knew it.

The road south from Agadir started promisingly as a highway, but soon petered out into a narrow, two-lane affair. There was little traffic, and it ran on between the desert and the ocean. From time to time I passed small fishing villages and herds of goats, but after a while there was nothing, just silence, thorn trees and the sound of the waves. Finally I came to a small bar hotel, standing on its own on the desert side of the road. Beyond was just more desert – this was the last place one could get a drink, or anything much, for hundreds of miles.

Perhaps it had been built to attract surfers, but there were none that I could see. The car park was empty except for an old van, and an older Toyota Land Cruiser. The words 'Bar Hotel' were painted on the bare cinder blocks, but the place did not seem to have a name as such. Inside it smelt of stale urine, and flies circled in the passage. It didn't take me long to find his room: it was the only one occupied, and dim wailing from a local radio station bled through the door, just this side of audible.

The door was not locked. It was such a flimsy thing there was little point. Pierre Antar was lying on the bed, staring at the ceiling. There was a blackened spoon on the bedside table, and a syringe, but otherwise the room was quite empty. For a moment, I thought I saw a look of vague disappointment cross his face, and then he just looked at me as if I was something faraway that was of no concern to him.

On the journey, certain questions had again been turning over in my mind. One of these was why Antar had pretended to be Moroccan for so many years, when he was in fact an Iraqi from Mosul who had lost his family to an American bomb in the first Gulf War. This was what I had heard from my friend in the State Department when, already fearing the worst, I had asked him to search their records on Antar. Another was whether I had walked into a trap – or was it my questions about Bowen that had set his plan in motion? Above all, I wanted to know who Antar had been working for, or whether he had acted alone, with Hadley as his only paid accomplice.

But looking at Antar lying there on the bed, it was as if I had never known the man at all. His expression said only that I was wasting my time. I saw he was unable to give me any answers because he was a blind instrument and nothing more. In that one moment, I think I doubted everything I had assumed, including my own sanity, and the next minute was the longest in my life. My back felt a mile wide as I walked back along the passage into the light. I ran to my car, and drove away from that moment as fast as I could.

Only a few months later, there would come the news of Hadley's death. It was a car crash, on the old beach highway between Marbella and Calahonda. This was a dangerous stretch of road, one of the worst in Europe; the locals called it the four-lane mortuary. No one seemed particularly surprised about the death, and it was not spoken about much.

Only a month after that, the rumours about Antar began going round. People said he had died in the back-streets of Agadir over a deal that had gone bad. He had been up to his old tricks, demanding samples on a deal that he never intended to see through; some said it was suicide, others that it was an overdose. All I can say is, from that time on Antar was not heard of again. Whether he was dead or not, no one could verify – all I know for sure is that no one has ever seen him since.

It felt as if hidden hands were cleaning up. Hadley probably never knew what he had gotten into, and in a sense Antar's motives were understandable – pure, almost. He had probably just wanted revenge for his family, killed by the American bomb, and I sensed a machine had been in motion from that day I had first heard about Bowen. The same set of images kept flickering through my head: Gordon Walker, standing with his cigar beside my pool; those three nondescript villas in those lanes filled with jasmine and bougainvillea; the pictures on the wall of Antar's cabin which looked like the streets of Tangiers, but weren't; Antar again, sobbing under the ruined building in

Cancelada; Hadley, nervous at the wheel of his camper van, that day outside my chalet.

If there was a pattern to it all, it would probably always remain slightly out of my reach and I would only ever glimpse oblique corners of it. My best guess was that the gear had been contaminated accidentally in one of the Brink's-Mat gang's smelting yards. These were highly toxic environments, and anything there would have become saturated by the noxious gases from the metals. It would not have been the first time something like this had happened, and the gang had probably been sitting on this gear for a long time, trying to work out a way of offloading it without selling it into their own home markets. Somehow, Antar must have heard about the gear, and when I had come looking for Bowen's stash, Antar's desire for revenge and the Brink's-Mat group's hunger for profit had converged.

When it came down to it, I had been no less blind about what I had really got into than Antar, maybe even more so. I braced myself for the worst, but the months passed without anything further happening. Perhaps my profile was too high to risk removing me from the stage, but more likely they just believed I did not know enough to pose a risk. I was content they should think that – and yet sometimes, even after all these years, when I think back to that time, I feel a faint pulse of the same fear. I know it will be with me until my final days. It made me realize that

I would have to leave this business for good. It was not worth risking my life for.

Over the next decade, I did my best to build a new life for myself, keen to move on and leave this difficult period behind me. I developed a new show and toured variations of it at Glastonbury and the other large festivals every summer; I dabbled in the legal high market, importing herbal tinctures from bushmen and specialist alternative practitioners in South Africa to sell at these festivals and online from a site based in Holland and run by an old friend. I researched the medicinal marijuana market, and held meetings with senior medical figures about the possibility of selling legal hemp products. Most of all, I kept moving and travelling, never staying in one place for more than a few days; over the decade I visited almost every country which would still permit me entry, including Taiwan, Colombia, Chile, Corsica, Holland, Germany, France, Ireland, the Caribbean and all the other South American countries, along with every corner of the British Isles multiple times. And yet in all this time, I couldn't quite shake the feeling that I was running away from something I would never escape, something that was already catching up with me.

In fact, it seemed my days were already numbered and the end was closer than I imagined. In the autumn of 2014, after experiencing gradually increasing general muscle pain and fatigue for several years, I received a diagnosis of inoperable cancer.

It was around this time that I had also heard the rumours of the deaths of Dennis Watkins and Elisabeth Dermot. All this time, it seemed, they had been living under assumed names in Goa, India. The body in the tunnel had not been Dermot's, after all, and was never positively identified. Perhaps her documents had been left on the body there so that it would be assumed she had died and she could lie low. With both her and Watkins now dead, no one was ever going to know for sure.

By this time the other main players – Jacobs, Purse, Roth and Salomon – had all also died or were sick with various forms of cancer, which I suspected might be related in some way also to their proximity to the toxic load. Although there was no way to prove this, it felt as if everyone who had come close to Bowen's stash had been doomed. I no longer felt I had much to fear, or lose, if I laid out the truth of what had happened. With each session of chemotherapy at the oncology department at St James's Hospital, it felt as if I was wrestling with the Minotaur and losing; but it would decrease my tumour load, and stabilize me sufficiently that I was able to begin to write this account of my years in Bowen's shadow. From now on it seemed the enemy would be something inside me, as implacable as anything I had ever faced, but I was determined to beat the odds, as I had, as much through the offices of luck as good planning, in the past and so set about changing my diet, eating non-acidic foods and drinking lemon juice each morning to cleanse my liver, cutting down my smoking and self-medicating with the best dope I could find. I was now looking forward to each day as never before and in a break between chemotherapy sessions I made it out to Ibiza for what I realized might be the last time, but of course hoped wouldn't be. The season had not started yet, and on the first night I went down to the beach below the Cafe del Mar building, not much of a beach to be honest, just some rocks and shingle and a few boats gently rocking in the swell; and looking out into the sunset with the lazy bars of chill-out guitar drifting through the warm air down the beach, never had it felt so good to be a survivor and alive for one more day.

ACKNOWLEDGEMENTS

There are so many people who have contributed to my having been able to write this book, either with their loving care or their tenacious diligence and stamina in getting the job done. It is difficult to single out specific individuals, but I have to.

I thank Patrick Walsh and all at Conville & Walsh for clinching the deal; Robin Harvie, Jamie Coleman and all at Pan Macmillan for taking the extraordinary risk of publishing it; for their painstaking attention to detail and for their stalwart patience throughout. I thank my thoroughly adored children – Patrick, Francesca, Amber and Myfanwy – who have been brilliant throughout and heroic in their care and attentions; all the friends and well-wishers whose love and kindness have kept me going; the beyond excellent Oncology Department at St James's hospital, Leeds; Alabama Three, Lynne Allbutt, Mark Badger, Dave Beer, Paul Betesh, Bez, Crofton Black, Tina Butler, Ray Carter, John Cooper Clark, Freddie Foreman, Chris Gascoigne, Bernie Davies, Martin Deeson, Hywell

Dinsdale, Ernie Eban, Carys Eleri, Ben Goldacre, Richard Gray, Peter Hook, Lord Jeremy Hutchinson Q.C., Rhys Ifans, Mick Jagger, David Jenkins, Jacob and Jo-Jo Kelly, Ned Kelly, Kermit Leveridge, Dan Macmillan, Cerys Matthews, Andrew Maxwell, Biff Mitchell, Elspeth Moore, Helen Peto, Jamie Peto, Professor Julian Peto, Rachel Peto, Professor Sir Richard Peto, Sassie Peto, Steve Pyke, David Robson, Rajah Singh, Penny Slinger, John Stein, Stereophonics, Super Furry Animals, Sara Louise Turner and Emma Wilkinson, Greg Wilson; Dan, my super-effective tour and event manager, and all at Get Involved Ltd, particularly John Hughes and Rob da Bank; all those who knew me at the time of the events of this book and are part of that era of my life, and without whom the world would be a smaller and sadder place; my old friend Tony H in Spain, the prompter in the shadows, without whom this project would not have been possible, and the one who knows where all the bodies are buried.

My sister, Linda, and my girlfriend, Caroline Brown, who continuously provide the perfection of care, warmth, love and tenderness.

Lastly and firstly, Irvine Welsh, whose inspirational writing enabled me and hundreds of others to have the courage to write about drugs.